Sainte-Beuve to Baudelaire

Sainte-Beuve to Baudelaire

A poetic legacy / by Norman H. Barlow

Duke University Press   Durham, N. C.   1964

Library of Congress Catalogue Card number 64-19697
Printed in the United States of America
by Heritage Printers, Inc., Charlotte, N. C.

Foreword

This volume is directed to those students of Baudelaire who, like the author, have been intrigued by the enigma of a poetic affinity between the creator of the *Fleurs du Mal* and the Romantic lyricist in Sainte-Beuve.

In order to conserve the time and energy of the reader, the following bibliographical procedures have been adopted:

Sainte-Beuve:

1. For the original *Poésies de Joseph Delorme,* citations are made from the texts established in Gérald Antoine's critical edition—*Vie, Poésies et Pensées de Joseph Delorme.* Paris: Nouvelles Editions Latines, 1956.

2. For the *Consolations,* the *Pensées d'août,* and other poems normally associated with Delorme, the reader is referred to the texts appearing in the second revised edition of the *Poésies complètes.* Paris: G. Charpentier, 1890.

3. For the novel *Volupté,* citations are made from the text in the 1890 edition. Paris: G. Charpentier.

Baudelaire:

1. For the verses addressed to Sainte-Beuve in 1844, citations are

made from the appropriate pages in *Juvenilia, œuvres posthumes, reliquiae.* Edited by Jacques Crépet. 3 vols. Paris: Louis Conard, 1939-1952.

2. For the *Fleurs du Mal*, citations are made from the texts appearing in the critical edition by Jacques Crépet and Georges Blin. Paris: José Corti, 1942.

3. For all other literary works, references are made to the texts as they appear in the *Œuvres complètes.* 2 vols. Paris: Le Club du Meilleur Livre, Le Nombre d'Or, 1955.

In addition, a restricted bibliography is furnished of works by other authors pertinent to the scope of the present study and to which references have been made in the text or in footnotes. However, for the most complete bibliography on Baudelaire, the reader is directed to W. T. Bandy's *Répertoire des Écrits sur Baudelaire* (Madison, Wis.: Privately printed, 1953), of which roneotyped copies are available. In regard to Sainte-Beuve, the best bibliography appears in Jean Bonnerot's *Un demi-siècle d'études sur Sainte-Beuve, 1904-1954* (Paris: Société d'édition "Les Belles Lettres," 1957).

For the initiation and completion of this study the author is immeasurably indebted to the encouragement of Professor Loring B. Walton and of other members past and present of the Department of Romance Languages at Duke University. Publication has been made possible by the interest and generosity of the Graduate Committee on Publications of Duke University.

N. H. B.

Contents

[*vii*]

Sainte-Beuve to Baudelaire

1. Introduction

Just two years before his death, Baudelaire addressed a letter to Sainte-Beuve (March 15, 1865) in which he offered this graceful recognition of his poetic debt to the elder poet-critic: "Décidément vous aviez raison: *Joseph Delorme*, c'est *Les Fleurs du Mal* de la veille. La comparaison est glorieuse pour moi. Vous aurez la bonté de ne pas la trouver offensante pour vous."[1] Sainte-Beuve accepted the acknowledgment before two weeks had passed:

> Mais vous êtes là avec un ami, Poulet-Malassis, et tous deux vous broyez ensemble de l'ennui, des rêves, de la poésie. Vous dites vrai: la mienne se rapprochait de la vôtre; j'avais goûté du même fruit amer, plein de cendre au fond. De là votre sympathie si aimable et si fidèle pour moi.[2]

1. Charles Baudelaire, *Correspondance générale*, Vol. V: *1865 et 1866*, ed. Jacques Crépet (Paris: Louis Conard, 1949), pp. 64-65.
2. Charles-Augustin Sainte-Beuve, *Correspondance: 1822-1865* (Paris: Calmann Lévy, 1877), I, 359-360.

This exchange between follower and precursor is the first indication that an extensive study of Sainte-Beuve's influence on Baudelaire might be fruitful. It is doubtful, however, whether the recognition and its acceptance would have been substantially rich enough to indicate the scope of a probable poetic legacy were it not for the existence of additional primary sources before and after the correspondence of 1865. Among these sources, the widest significance is to be found in verses of a poem addressed to Sainte-Beuve by Baudelaire in 1844:

> Ce fut dans ce conflit de molles circonstances,
> Mûri par vos sonnets, préparé par vos stances,
> Qu'un soir, ayant flairé le livre et son esprit,
> J'emportai sur mon cœur l'histoire d'Amaury.
> Tout abîme mystique est à deux pas du doute.—
> Le breuvage infiltré lentement, goutte à goutte,
> En moi qui, dès quinze ans, vers le gouffre entraîné,
> Déchiffrais couramment les soupirs de René,
> Et que de l'inconnu la soif bizarre alterre [*sic*]
> —A travaillé le fond de la plus mince artère.—[3]

These lines obviously refer to the period of adolescence, to the time of physiological and psychological crisis in youth; but the date 1844 is important. By that time Baudelaire is credited with having composed many of his *Fleurs du Mal*. Yet the abnormally mature poet at this point in his career admits with striking clarity his kinship to Joseph Delorme and to the Amaury of Sainte-Beuve's *Volupté*. It is an avowal which could be supported only many years later when Sainte-Beuve was able to judge the over-all tone of the *Fleurs du Mal* in relation to his own poetry. However, Sainte-Beuve's subsequent admission of kinship, in his letter presumably written on July 20,

3. Charles Baudelaire, "Poésie," *Juvenilia, œuvres posthumes, reliquiae*, ed. Jacques Crépet (Paris: Louis Conard, 1939), I, 15-17.

[4]

1857, was vague and lukewarm, giving no indication that he had understood any aesthetic unity in his disciple's creation.[4] In this communication he admitted in common with Baudelaire only the narrow choice of lyric themes by which both had been restricted in their poetic production. Noting that Baudelaire had emphasized the most satanic aspects of man's spiritual anguish, Sainte-Beuve pointed out that he himself had set a previous example in the Delorme poems. Observing further that his subsequent *Consolations* were inspired by a gentler and purer tone, he advised Baudelaire to seek a similar development. However, the ambiguous nature of Sainte-Beuve's response—an ambiguity re-emphasized in his article on Baudelaire of January 20, 1862—seemed not to diminish the ardent admiration of the young poet for the "Rayons jaunes" and *Volupté*, expressed in his letter of January 25, 1862.[5]

Finally, the most fruitful acknowledgment of the older poet's influence is to be found in Baudelaire's letter to Sainte-Beuve of January 15, 1866,[6] late in the poet's life when his sincerity is least questionable. In this letter Baudelaire pointed out the natural coincidence of the *Poésies de Joseph Delorme* with his own prose poems, the *Spleen de Paris*. For him there was indeed in this parallel an invariable element peculiar to his own temperament. He went so far as to specify a dozen poems that he especially admired. These were chosen not only from the Delorme poems but also from the *Consolations* and the *Pensées d'août*. In this same expansive letter, Baudelaire deemed the latter collection of verse worthy of the genre *élégie analytique*, and the *Poésies de Joseph Delorme* he specified as *poèmes parisiens*.

The exchanges reported above form the dramatic elements in a mystery which exercised the professional curiosity of

4. Sainte-Beuve, *Correspondance: 1822-1865*, I, 219-222.
5. Baudelaire, *Correspondance générale*, IV, 45-46.
6. Baudelaire, *ibid.*, V, 214-218.

historians of French literature during the second half of the nineteenth century and has elicited a lively interest in the present century. "Mystery" describes a problem created by Baudelaire's failure—for unknown reasons inherent in the tempest of his life—to undertake a more detailed study or evaluation of Sainte-Beuve's poetry. An item listed among his prose works in 1866 under the title "Sainte-Beuve ou Joseph Delorme jugé par l'auteur des *Fleurs du Mal*"[7] was never discovered by the editors of the posthumous editions. Even more frustrating for scholarly research is Sainte-Beuve's extreme reservation in his evaluation of the *Fleurs du Mal*, or indeed of Baudelaire's other literary works. Fernand Vandérem has presented this reservation of the elder poet in a most unfavorable light as professional malice, basing his contention on the history of the curiously strained relations between precursor and follower.[8] This history, whether seen through Vandérem or through Sainte-Beuve's definitive biographer, André Billy,[9] casts a shadow of insincerity over the formula of influence emerging from the correspondence of 1865.

Nevertheless, the basic propositions of the correspondence are supported by the purely circumstantial evidence derived from the place of the two poets in the literary history of the period. If there were some qualities in Sainte-Beuve the innovator that attracted Baudelaire, they may perhaps best be explained by a glance at the elder poet's own particular entry into the arena of Romantic lyricism. By his own account the gate was narrow and the field of poetic distinction was largely occupied by three poetic giants, Lamartine, Hugo, and Vigny, who were struggling mightily to continue the work of André Chénier in giving new life to the fading poetry of the Classical schools. Of these giants, the reign of Lamartine was succeeded

7. *Ibid.*, V, 250.
8. Fernand Vandérem, *Baudelaire et Sainte-Beuve* (Paris: H. Leclerc, 1917).
9. André Billy, *Sainte-Beuve, sa vie et son temps*, Vol. II: *L'épicurien*, 1848-1869 (Paris: Flammarion, 1952), pp. 94-117.

by the empire of Hugo, while the introverted Vigny retired soon to his ivory tower. Sainte-Beuve saw the restricted field of his own poetic inspiration as in marked contrast with the lofty soarings of the lyric veterans. He presented the antithesis in a section of the poem "A M. Villemain," written in 1838, where the images recall the apparent paradox of Baudelaire's title, *Fleurs du Mal:*

> On raconte qu'au sein d'une des Pyramides,
> Aussi haut que la cime atteint aux cieux splendides,
> Aussi profond s'enfonce et plonge dans les flancs,
> Sous le roc de la base et les sables brûlants,
> Un puits mystérieux, dont la pointe qui sonde,
> A défaut de soleil, s'en va ressaisir l'onde.
> En ce puits, s'il n'avait pour couvercle d'airain,
> Pour sépulcre éternel, son granit souverain,
> On verrait en plein jour malgré l'heure étonnée,
> La nuit dans sa fraîcheur se mirer couronnée.
> Si les cieux défendus manquent à notre essor,
> Perçons, perçons la terre, on les retrouve encor![10]

The muse who inhabited those nether regions certainly did not belong to the first Romantic generation in France:

> Bien; il faut l'aigle aux monts, le géant à l'abîme,
> Au sublime spectacle un spectateur sublime.
> Moi, j'aime à cheminer et je reste plus bas.
> Quoi? des rocs, des forêts, des fleuves? . . . oh! non pas,
> Mais bien moins; mais un champ, un peu d'eau qui murmure,
> Un vent frais agitant une grêle ramure;
> L'étang sous la bruyère avec le jonc qui dort; . . .[11]

10. Charles-Augustin Sainte-Beuve, *Poésies complètes* (2nd ed. rev.; Paris: G. Charpentier, 1890), pp. 378-379.
11. Charles-Augustin Sainte-Beuve, *Vie, Poésies et Pensées de Joseph Delorme,* ed. Gérald Antoine (Paris: Nouvelles Editions Latines, 1956), pp. 78-79.

In one of his *Causeries du lundi*, Sainte-Beuve demonstrated in 1854 a strong interest in the intimate poetry favored by the English Lake School of Romantic poets.[12] Maxwell Austin Smith points out that the French poet, in his role as literary critic, assumed the obligation to introduce into France the domestic intimacy for which William Cowper was already renowned in England.[13] This fervor for the intimate genre in English Romanticism was no doubt connected with the restricted field of lyric inspiration in which Sainte-Beuve found himself.

In a letter to Baudelaire, dated presumably July 20, 1857,[14] he made an unusually open comparison of his own poetic inspiration with that of the younger poet. This communication sheds some light on the enforced restriction, common to both men, of the fields of poetic creation. The letter is often linked, though incorrectly,[15] with the *Articles justificatifs*, presented as a memorandum to the presiding judge by Baudelaire on the occasion of his trial in 1857 for offenses against public morality. Sainte-Beuve professed to understand how the author of the *Fleurs du Mal* had been driven to seek his poetic substance in the diabolic. Yet in the wisdom of his own experience, the elder poet warned Baudelaire against the unrelieved darkness of his pessimism, against the absence of any spiritual resurrection:

> Vous dites quelque part, en marquant le réveil spirituel qui se fait le matin après les nuits mal passées, que, lorsque "l'aube blanche et vermeille," se montrant tout à coup, apparaît en compagnie de "l'idéal rongeur," à ce moment, par une sorte d'expiation vengeresse, "Dans la brute assoupie

12. Charles-Augustin Sainte-Beuve, *Les causeries du lundi* (Paris: Garnier Frères, 1857-1872), XI, 121.

13. Maxwell Austin Smith, *L'influence des Lakistes sur les romantiques français* (Paris: Jouve et Cie, 1920), pp. 91-92.

14. Sainte-Beuve, *Correspondance: 1822-1865*, I, 219-222.

15. Charles Baudelaire, *Œuvres complètes* (Paris: Le Club du Meilleur Livre, *Le Nombre d'Or*, 1955), II, 1229. Editor's note.

[8]

un ange se réveille!" C'est cet ange que j'invoque en vous et qu'il faut cultiver. Que si vous l'eussiez fait intervenir un peu plus souvent, en deux ou trois endroits bien distincts, cela eût suffi pour que votre pensée se dégageât, pour que tous ces rêves, toutes ces formes obscures et tous ces bizarres entrelacements où s'est lassée votre fantaisie, parussent dans leur vrai jour, c'est-à-dire à demi dispersés déjà et prêts à s'enfuir devant la lumière. Votre livre alors eût offert comme une "Tentation de saint Antoine," au moment où l'aube approche et où l'on sent qu'elle va cesser.

Citing his own example as pertinent to the younger poet's situation, Sainte-Beuve then pointed out that the *Consolations*, by their calmer and purer tone, obtained a measure of pardon for the virulence of the *Poésies de Joseph Delorme*. He continued with a warning against the excessive intellectuality of the *Fleurs du Mal*, thereby unintentionally emphasizing the excessive sentimentality of his own *Pensées d'août*:

Vous vous défiez trop de la passion, c'est chez vous une théorie. Vous accordez trop à l'esprit, à la combinaison. Laissez-vous faire, ne craignez pas tant de sentir comme les autres, n'ayez jamais peur d'être trop commun; vous aurez toujours assez, dans votre finesse d'expression, de quoi vous distinguer.

Much of the matter in this important letter was condensed in the *Petits moyens de défense tels que je les conçois*, which Sainte-Beuve prepared for Baudelaire's trial:

Tout était pris dans le domaine de la poésie.
Lamartine avait pris les *cieux*, Victor Hugo avait pris la *terre*, et plus que la terre. Laprade avait pris les *forêts*. Musset avait pris la passion et l'orgie éblouissante. D'autres avaient pris le *foyer*, la *vie rurale*, etc.
Théophile Gautier avait pris l'Espagne et ses hautes couleurs. Que restait-il?
Ce que Baudelaire a pris.
Il y a été comme forcé.[16]

16. *Ibid.*, II, 1177.

In comparison to the letter of 1857 just examined, there was a much more equivocal evaluation of the disciple's poetry in Sainte-Beuve's article appearing in the *Nouveaux lundis* of January 20, 1862, in which Baudelaire appears isolated on a peninsula of abnormal Romantic bizarreness:

> Il n'est pas si aisé qu'on le croirait de prouver à des académiciens politiques et hommes d'Etat comme quoi il y a, dans les *Fleurs du Mal*, des pièces très remarquables vraiment pour le talent et pour l'art; de leur expliquer que, dans les petits poèmes en prose de l'auteur, "le Vieux Saltimbanque" et "les Veuves" sont deux bijoux, et qu'en somme M. Baudelaire a trouvé moyen de se bâtir, à l'extrémité d'une langue de terre réputée inhabitable et par delà les confins du romantisme connu, un kiosque bizarre, fort orné, fort tourmenté, mais coquet et mystérieux, où on lit de l'Edgar Poe, où l'on récite des sonnets exquis, où l'on s'enivre avec le haschich pour en raisonner après, où l'on prend de l'opium et mille drogues abominables dans des tasses d'une porcelaine achevée. Ce singulier kiosque, fait en marqueterie, d'une originalité concertée et composite, qui, depuis quelque temps, attire les regards à la pointe extrême du Kamchatka romantique, j'appelle cela *la folie Baudelaire*.[17]

It is a point of historical interest that Victor Hugo was moved to much the same professional feeling by both Sainte-Beuve and Baudelaire. Hugo defined his conception of Sainte-Beuve's style in his speech celebrating the elder poet's admission to the French Academy: "Vous avez su dans le demi-jour découvrir un sentier qui est le vôtre et créer une élégie qui est vous-même. Vous avez su donner à certains épanchements de l'âme un accent nouveau."[18] The "accent nouveau" becomes "frisson nouveau" in Hugo's encouraging letter to Baudelaire of October 6, 1859:

17. Charles-Augustin Sainte-Beuve, *Les nouveaux Lundis* (Paris: Calmann Lévy, 1890), I, 401.
18. André Billy, *Sainte-Beuve, sa vie et son temps*, Vol. I: *Le romantique 1804-1848* (Paris: Flammarion, 1952), pp. 74-75.

Que faites-vous quand vous écrivez ces vers saisissants: *"les Sept Vieillards"* et *"les Petites Vieilles,"* que vous me dédiez et dont je vous remercie? Que faites-vous? Vous marchez. Vous dotez le ciel de l'art d'on ne sait quel rayon macabre. Vous créez un frisson nouveau.[19]

If Sainte-Beuve's influence on Baudelaire's lyric inspiration is to be chronologically significant in the development of French poetry, it is necessary to fix the period of his disciple's poetic formation. Ernest Prarond, his collaborator at the time in a group of novice poets known as the *École Normande,* stated that some twenty of the future *Fleurs du Mal* were composed before the end of 1843.[20] He recalled hearing parts of many others at the same period, some included in the *Fleurs* of 1857 and some not appearing in any edition known to him. In venturing a time limit to Baudelaire's apprenticeship, I have established the *Limbes* of 1851 as the first series of his poems Baudelaire credited with having a dominating motif. Through many stages of refinement and with many additions, though scarcely any longer at the hands of a novice, these *Limbes,* an early chronicle of modern anguish, became the first edition of the *Fleurs du Mal,* the artistic unity of which is based upon an aesthetic of evil. It will be shown later in this chapter that the period of serious production attested by Prarond was not much later than that which marked the height of Baudelaire's declared interest in Sainte-Beuve's lyrical works.

As he composed his earlier poems, the disciple strove to transform the synthesis of lyric themes offered in the Beuvean legacy into a poetry of modernity more consistent with his own relatively advanced theory of art. His aim was an aesthetic blending of subjective effusion with the objective realism of contemporary life. Many of the problems that he encountered

19. Victor Hugo, *Correspondance: 1836-1882* (Paris: Calmann Lévy, 1898), p. 226.
20. Baudelaire, *Œuvres complètes,* II, 1154-1155.

in the composition of the *Fleurs du Mal* as an aesthetic unity were related to his search for the true poetic expression of modern man. By 1846 Baudelaire the novice had come to define Romanticism as "l'expression la plus récente, la plus actuelle du Beau."[21] The philosophy of progress had convinced him that there were as many idealizations upon life as there were ways for human individuals to comprehend morality, love, religion, and other vital experiences. Thus, Romanticism did not consist of any absolute idealization of a given subject, but rather of a conception of that subject governed by the ethical system or moral philosophy in any particular age. His great contribution to poetic modernism was his insistence upon a rational and historic theory of beauty, which presented beauty not as one and absolute but as endowed with a double composition. This duality included both an eternal and invariable element, of a size difficult to determine, and a relative, circumstantial element, which was the age, the fashion, the morality, the passion—in brief, the historical situation in time and space. Without the relative element, the absolute element in a subject of beauty was indigestible for human nature. Baudelaire saw the duality of art implied by this theory as an inevitable consequence of the spiritual dichotomy in man. The permanent element in beauty could be considered as the soul of any artistic creation, the variable element as its body. For the painter of modernity, argued Baudelaire, it was a question of separating the poetic from the historical and contemporary, of drawing eternal values from the transient phenomena of life. Modernity was thus to be defined as the transient, the fleeting, the accidental—that half of art which supplements the eternal and immutable.[22] In the *Salon de 1846*, speaking as a critic of the visual arts, Baudelaire maintained that the epic aspect of modern life was demonstrated

21. Baudelaire, "Le Salon de 1846," *ibid.*, I, 221.
22. Baudelaire, "Le peintre de la vie moderne," *ibid.*, II, 587-588, 597-598.

in just this separation of the poetic from the historical or incidental. In the process of poetic creation, absolute beauty was to be skimmed from the surface of all incidental beauty. The particular quality of every immediate beauty arose from the human passions peculiar to each individual. In naming Sainte-Beuve "poète parisien," Baudelaire was remembering that Paris had always seemed especially rich in that historical reality from which the poetry of modern heroism might be distilled. He had observed elsewhere in that same *Salon*:

> Le spectacle de la vie élégante et des milliers d'existences flottantes qui circulent dans les souterrains d'une grande ville,—criminels et filles entretenues,—*la Gazette des Tribunaux*, et *le Moniteur* nous prouvent que nous n'avons qu'à ouvrir les yeux pour connaître notre héroïsme.

> La vie parisienne est féconde en sujets poétiques et merveilleux. Le merveilleux nous enveloppe et nous abreuve comme l'atmosphère; mais nous ne le voyons pas.[23]

The poetic potential of incidental reality is well summarized by the formula of true aesthetics presented in Baudelaire's *Salon de 1859*:

> Tout l'univers visible n'est qu'un magasin d'images et de signes auxquels l'imagination donnera une place et une valeur relative; c'est une espèce de pâture que l'imagination doit digérer et transformer. Toutes les facultés de l'âme humaine doivent être subordonnées à l'imagination, qui les met en réquisition toutes à la fois.[24]

For the poet, the mere recording of historical reality is a futile activity of the positivist who seeks to represent things as they would be in a world where man and his interpretive powers do not exist.[25] The artistic imagination, on the other hand, analyzes the immediate reality of "tout l'univers visible" in a system of mathematically precise symbols which relate all the

---

23. Baudelaire, "Le Salon de 1846," *ibid.*, I, 301-302.
24. Baudelaire, "Le Salon de 1859," *ibid.*, II, 132.
25. *Ibid.*, II, 133.

different phenomena in one universal analogy.[26] These symbols are then related to the Divine Absolute by the metaphysical tendency of artistic creation. Baudelaire's own notes on Edgar Allan Poe establish this tendency toward the supernatural as the very principle of poetry:

> Ainsi, le principe de la poésie est, strictement et simplement, l'aspiration humaine vers une beauté supérieure, et la manifestation de ce principe est dans un enthousiasme, une excitation de l'âme,—enthousiasme tout à fait indépendant de la passion qui est l'ivresse du cœur, et de la vérité qui est la pâture de la raison.[27]

The distant harmonies of the "analogie universelle" had been heard by Sainte-Beuve, too, in what might be called his poetics—the *Pensées de Joseph Delorme*. In *Pensée XX* he had discussed the function of symbol in the artist's special perception of life.[28] For Delorme, artistic feeling implied a keen and intimate feeling for objective reality. With "la clef des symboles et l'intelligence des figures" as his birthright, the lyric poet recognized what was incoherent and contradictory to ordinary men as "un contraste harmonique, un accord à distance sur la lyre universelle." The providential gift of artistic perception was again affirmed by the elder poet in one of his *Consolations*, "A mon ami Leroux."[29] In this poem, in keeping with the Christian tone of the collection, the artist sees the innumerable forms of matter as the expression of divine thought, which cannot be enclosed in the finite. Thus a direct metaphysical translation is made from the system of analogy operating in the created universe to the infinite reality of God the Creator. In his novel *Volupté*, Sainte-Beuve used the same system of correspondences to illustrate the nourishment of

26. Baudelaire, "Victor Hugo," *ibid.*, II, 478.
27. Baudelaire, "Notices sur Poe," *ibid.*, I, 645.
28. Sainte-Beuve, *Poésies complètes*, pp. 157-158.
29. *Ibid.*, p. 244.

man's life by spiritually significant thought.[30] The hero, Amaury, meditates upon the moral meaning of some "pensée d'harmonie, de beauté, de tristesse, d'attendrissement, d'austérité ou d'admiration" lying beneath all the works and beings of the universe. In contemplating the phenomena of the physical world, he feels able to interpret the various signs as fragments of a divine unity.

The truly lyrical inspiration of the poetic state, as Baudelaire wrote in his article on Théodore de Banville, is a manner of feeling in universal terms, a potential expansion of the soul into some loftier spiritual experience than is yielded by the crudities of exterior reality. Yet lyrical feeling, when it operates upon the historic or fugitive aspect of that same exterior reality, creates a suggestive magic which is the essence of poetic modernism.[31] In another study on modernity in art, Baudelaire stated that this magic embraces both exterior reality and the subjective reality of the artist.[32] To emphasize introspection as a primary source of lyrical expression, he offered the following definition of Romanticism in the arts: "Qui dit romantisme, dit art moderne,—c'est-à-dire intimité, spiritualité, couleur, aspiration vers l'infini, exprimées par tous les moyens que contiennent les arts."[33] There is no better interpretation of this formula than the commentary of Jean Massin, who explains:

> Intimité: pénétration des tendances profondes de l'homme. Spiritualité: origine et valeur religieuse de ces tendances. Couleur: vibration chaude et vivante du cœur intime. Aspiration vers l'infini: ces tendances elles-mêmes et le mouvement de notre âme vers Dieu.[34]

Among the critics who have concerned themselves with the

---

30. Charles-Augustin Sainte-Beuve, *Volupté* (Paris: G. Charpentier, 1890), p. 160.
31. Baudelaire, "Théodore de Banville," *Œuvres complètes*, II, 511-517.
32. Baudelaire, "L'art philosophique," *ibid.*, II, 193.
33. Baudelaire, "Le Salon de 1846," *ibid.*, I, 221.
34. Jean Massin, *Baudelaire "entre Dieu et Satan"* (Paris: René Julliard, 1945), p. 57.

application of Baudelaire's poetics of universal analogy to his *Fleurs du Mal*, Judd David Hubert, in his study *L'esthétique des Fleurs du Mal*, offers in my opinion the clearest exposition of the Baudelairean poetic order. Hubert insists on the distinction between the function and the meaning of each element in a poem.[35] Maintaining that the poet as creator is primarily interested in functions, he uses a simultaneous multiplicity of meanings which emphasize the contribution of each poetic element to the aesthetic unity of the poem and of each poem to the unity of the collection. Such an approach is supported by Baudelaire's own claim for the unity of his *Fleurs*.[36] Particularly in the "Tableaux parisiens," Hubert's use of the "ambiguïté surnaturaliste" facilitates the distillation of Baudelaire's "merveilleux" from the crude natural reality of metropolitan life.[37] Hence, for the Parisian poems, and elsewhere in the *Fleurs*, I have not hesitated to use this critic's interpretations, wherever they seem to aid in isolating the creator's poetic objective more clearly from the mere meaning of incidental reality.

In their poetics, both Sainte-Beuve and Baudelaire demonstrated their theoretical acceptance of a twofold system of analogy, which includes both the terrestrial and the transcendental. In his study on Baudelaire's poetic universe, Lloyd James Austin applies the term *symbolisme* only to the first component. For the second he uses *symbolique*. Without entering into Austin's argument as to the divine or satanic orientation of Baudelaire's original transcendental system, I share this scholar's view that a man-centered *symbolisme* is pre-eminent in the poet's artistic creation. Austin concluded that Baudelaire's poetry ultimately leads back to the lyrical expression of man's soul. Even if the infernal seems to have

35. Judd David Hubert, *L'esthétique des Fleurs du Mal* (Geneva: Pierre Cailler, 1953), p. 26.
36. Baudelaire, *Correspondance générale*, IV, 9.
37. Hubert, pp. 36-37.

the lion's share in the transcendental *symbolique*, a purely human system of symbols is basic to the unity of the poet's masterpiece.[38]

After duly considering rather sparse primary sources, the situation of the two poets in the development of French literature, and the convincing textual evidence of their parallel theories in poetics, the present study still embarks from a position on the periphery of a formidable, if provocative, enigma. Since the formula—*"Les Fleurs du Mal de la veille"*— was offered in 1865, almost a century of literary history has passed, and Baudelaire is now generally regarded as one of the great poets of modern world literature. Certain that only a careful exploration of the relevant texts can afford a measure of the reality which lies behind the mystery, I nevertheless have been fortified by the opinions of literary historians and critics over the years concerning the aesthetic affinity between the two poets. The most important of these are to be found in the writings of such notable scholars as Charpentier, Ferran, Thibaudet, Chérix, Prévost, and Ruff.[39] In their various ways, they have all pointed to a common engagement in the spiritual dilemma of modern youth and to a delicate perception of the moral paradox involved in the Romantic anguish of their day. The potential scope of a Beuvean legacy in lyrical inspiration is most clearly and concisely summarized by Thibaudet, who describes the affinity of the two poets by means of a threefold

38. Lloyd James Austin, *L'univers poétique de Baudelaire: symbolisme et symbolique* (Paris: Mercure de France, 1956), pp. 55-57, 134-135.

39. John Charpentier, *Évolution de la poésie lyrique de Joseph Delorme à Paul Claudel* (Paris: Œuvres représentatives, 1930), pp. 46-47, 51-52. André Ferran, *L'esthétique de Baudelaire* (Paris: Hachette, 1933), pp. 95-96. Albert Thibaudet, *Histoire de la littérature française de 1789 à nos jours* (Paris: Librairie Stock, 1936), pp. 321-323. Robert-Benoît Chérix, *Commentaire des Fleurs du Mal* (Geneva: Pierre Cailler, 1949), pp. 317, 319. Jean Prévost, *Baudelaire* (Paris: Mercure de France, 1953), p. 20. Marcel A. Ruff, *L'esprit du mal et l'esthétique baudelairienne* (Paris: Armand Colin, 1955), pp. 106-108, 110, 116, 158-160. Marcel A. Ruff, *Baudelaire: l'homme et l'œuvre* (Paris: Hatier-Boivin, 1955), pp. 10-11.

formula. The first element of this formula, "christianisme intérieur," implies a Christian consciousness of original sin. The second, "intelligence critique," suggests a wide moral perspicacity. The third element, "sentiment aigu de Paris," is related to the two preceding, in the sense that the moral tragedies of a great city are an exteriorization of the individual tragedy of spiritual duality. I feel that only a bold synthesis of aesthetic impression can form a reliable basis for Baudelaire's undiminished enthusiasm, as late as 1866, for the works of Sainte-Beuve. Happily, it is to such a synthesis that I have been led by the recent expressions of scholarly and critical opinion.

The choice of Sainte-Beuve's lyrical works appropriate to this examination follows Baudelaire's own directive—his poem dedicated to the elder poet in 1844 and already cited among the primary sources. Describing his own involvement in the anguish of his generation, the disciple refers to his preparation for moral awareness by his reading of Sainte-Beuve. By the logic of this poem in its entirety, the "conflit de molles circonstances," in which Baudelaire admits his own engagement, appears to refer to the psychological and physiological disequilibrium attendant upon adolescence and early manhood. His taste for Sainte-Beuve's writings thus was probably acquired during the period 1838-1841, which included his enrollment at the Collège Louis le Grand and his stay at the Pension Bailly et Lévêque prior to his voyage to the Indian Ocean in June, 1841. The experiences absorbed from the reading of "l'histoire d'Amaury" (*Volupté*) already suggest an embryonic awareness of spiritual ambivalence:

> J'en ai tout absorbé, les miasmes, les parfums,
> Le doux chuchotement des souvenirs défunts,
> Les longs enlacements des phrases symboliques,
> —Chapelets murmurants de madrigaux mystiques;
> —Livre voluptueux, si jamais il en fut.[40]

40. Baudelaire, *Juvenilia*, I, 17.

Baudelaire's introduction to *Volupté*—"mûri par vos sonnets, préparé par vos stances"—implies inspiration from the three published collections of Sainte-Beuve which would have been available to the young poet: the *Poésies de Joseph Delorme*, 1829; the *Consolations*, 1830; the *Pensées d'août*, 1838. The implication is supported by Baudelaire himself in the mention of poems from all three collections in his letter of January 15, 1866.[41] The effects of a Beuvean legacy in lyrical expression seem to have continued beyond the novice's departure for exotic lands in June, 1841, and his return to France in 1842, for Baudelaire observes, in further lines from the verses to Sainte-Beuve of 1844:

> Et depuis, soit au fond d'un asyle touffu,
> Soit que, sous les soleils des zônes différentes,
> L'Eternel bercement des houles enivrantes,
> Et l'aspect renaissant des horizons sans fin
> Ramenassent ce cœur vers le songe divin,—
> Soit dans les lourds loisirs d'un jour caniculaire,
> Ou dans l'oisiveté frileuse de frimaire,—
> Sous les flots du Tabac qui masque le plafond,
> J'ai partout feuilleté le mystère profond
> De ce livre si cher aux âmes engourdies
> Que leur destin marqua des mêmes maladies, . . .[42]

The Beuvean legacy defined in Thibaudet's concise formula is partially announced in the vague phraseology of the poem above, but the thematic elements involved have still to be tested in a comparative analysis. The purpose of these tests is to demonstrate in the work of both poets a common aesthetic synthesis which is based on their consciousness of man's spiritual scission.

41. Baudelaire, *Correspondance générale*, V, 214-218.
42. Baudelaire, *Juvenilia*, I, 17.

2. The elegy of modern anguish—Les Poésies de Joseph Delorme

The *Vie de Joseph Delorme*, which served as a prologue to the Delorme poems, announced the portrayal of yet another victim of the *mal du siècle*, which had ravaged the well-being and the life itself of many a young romanticist in nineteenth-century France. The French literary history of the period was almost dominated by analyses of this affliction; for many writers experienced in their personal lives the tragic frustration which formed the elegiac element in their art. Few of Sainte-Beuve's contemporaries failed to indentify the fictitious Delorme with the real author. Indeed, his biographer Billy notes that the erstwhile poet was still conscious at the age of fifty-three of leading a fateful existence true to the elegiac idiom of the Romantic hero.[1] Except for an obstinately persistent eighteenth-century rationalism peculiar to Sainte-Beuve rather than typical of the *mal du siècle*, the real Joseph Delorme represented, during his poetic period, a true child of the times.

1. Billy, *Sainte-Beuve*, I, 76.

By 1838, his adolescence already disturbed by personal anxieties, the precociously sensitive Baudelaire was bound to have been impressed by the sense of personal catastrophe conveyed in the Delorme poems. His burden of physical and material suffering was not yet heavy, but he increased it vicariously by absorbing Sainte-Beuve's elegiac poetry. Ultimately, both poets observed their personal failures from a remarkably similar point of view. Both the *Poésies de Joseph Delorme* and the *Fleurs du Mal* expressed the anguish of the gifted artist driven both by a persistent urge toward the transcendental ideal and by an intuitive perception of the universal analogy. They described the painful conflicts of genius with earthly society, its deceptions and disillusionment at the hands of fellow mortals, its unsuccessful search for absolute happiness in terms of mortal life with resulting bitterness in heart and soul. To compare the tone of the two works is by no means to ignore the obvious superiority of the *Fleurs* to the Delorme collection in both psychological and aesthetic unity. Regardless of the quality of their composition and arrangement, however, a moral portrait does begin to emerge from the *Poésies de Joseph Delorme* which is completed in the *Consolations*. At this point we are interested in the signs of spiritual consciousness discernible in this portrait; since it is upon such evidence, and on similar indications in the portrait of Sainte-Beuve's Amaury, that the validity of a substantial Beuvean legacy rests.

The essence of the Romantic elegy from Delorme's point of view is stated with sober economy in the poem "Le songe." Like the torchbearer of ancient Olympiads, youth carries into the arena of life the flame of its ambition. Destiny appears to smile upon its visions of glory, and it is quickly intoxicated by all that life seems to offer. But the early dreams of resounding action, love, and artistic fulfillment vanish with experience. When the naïve child is awakened from his dream of pure felicity by the harsh light of worldly reality, the torch of his

aspiration henceforth illuminates only his defeat and the unending tediousness of his existence. His illusion is dispersed in
the tears of his disenchantment. The basis of Delorme's elegiac
mood is thus a sense of deprivation: the loss of, or failure to
attain, both the worldly and the transcendental treasures of
human life; the wasting of energy in striving for ill-chosen objectives; and the worship of false idols. Among these idols, the
poet counts love not least, for in its more spiritual form it provides some satisfaction of his need for the ideal. Yet the purity
of young love, destined to be lost or perhaps never known, may
fall victim to the temptation of a sensual passion that bears its
own disenchantment. Thereafter, the orgies of the senses can
be halted only by angelic voices, by time, or by death. With
the years comes the need for serenity in love or in art, or even
for a meaningful life beyond the grave. The phenomenon of
the Romantic *mal du siècle* may be visualized, in the case of
Sainte-Beuve's hero, as a hopeful upward movement toward
fusion in the ideal, countered by an anticlimactic downward
curve of disillusionment and despair. The descent from the
original high objective imparts the halftones of a pale irony
to many of the loves of Delorme, loves of negation or compensation under the menace of old age and death.

In the poem "Premier amour" the youthful ideal of innocent
purity is presented as the source of Delorme's will to live.
When the hope of happiness is shattered by the young girl's
marriage to another, her deprived adorer seeks in the supernatural glow of her memory a spiritual consolation which is
distinctly Platonic:

> Qu'en silence adorant ta mémoire si chère,
> Je l'invoque en mes jours de faiblesse et d'ennui;
> Tel en sa sœur aînée un frère cherche appui,
> Tel un fils orphelin appelle encor sa mère.

The Platonic adoration of feminine purity is continued in

"Le dernier vœu," where the ugliness of the lover's physical affliction is contrasted with the splendor of a beautiful woman. The silent and unobtrusive worship of the beloved must henceforth be expressed in protective vigil and prayer.

Hardly a man, Delorme finds himself abandoned alike by love and the glory promised in patriotic service.[2] His youthfully ardent desires fettered by poverty, he learns to limit his ambition to a frugally simple life in some remote country cottage. There, his innocent leisure will be charmed by study and by the warm solace of male companionship.[3] But this humble dream does not long satisfy the youth who had dreamed of glory. His burning desires begin to seek distraction, even satisfaction, in the indulgence of the flesh. The tranquillity of learning and obscurity yields to the erotic intoxication inspired by the physical charms of the first in a series of fatal Helens.[4] In her successor he finds the body more attractive by far than the mind. It is to this "belle Ignorante" that he gives the key to his prison of anxiety, for carnal passion contains its own mysticism:

> Qu'est toute la science auprès d'un sein pâmé,
> Et d'une bouche en proie au baiser enflammé,
> Et d'une voix qui pleure et chante à l'agonie?
>
> Ton frais regard console en un jour nébuleux;
> On lit son avenir au fond de tes yeux bleus,
> Et ton sourire en sait plus long que le génie.[5]

These priestesses of sensual passion, as Delorme confesses in the poem "En m'en revenant un soir d'été vers neuf heures et demie," really only simulate an understanding of poetic genius. For all its mystical potential, physical love does not suffice to

2. Sainte-Beuve, *Vie, Poésies et Pensées de Joseph Delorme*, ed. Antoine, p. 34.
3. *Ibid.*, p. 35.
4. *Ibid.*, p. 51.
5. *Ibid.*, p. 123.

dispel the poet's essentially metaphysical anxieties. More insistent than carnal "volupté," a voice calls from beyond the
worldly life to interrupt the hero in the satisfaction of his
profane appetites. Under its persuasion, the too facile pleasures
of the flesh in the poem "Le rendez-vous" become meaningless:

> Malgré les doux serments relus dans sa prunelle,
> Les baisers, les grands bras prêts à me retenir,
> Demain, je sortirai pour ne plus revenir;
> Car je foule la fleur sitôt qu'elle est ravie,
> Et mon bonheur, à moi, n'est pas de cette vie.

In the verses "A Alfred de M." the same supernatural voice,
communicated through Delorme's moral intelligence, halts
him on the very threshold of triumphant desire. The innocence
of youth confronts for the first time the sensuous enchantment
of carnal forms. The intoxication of desire, be it for woman's
flesh or worldly glory, finds all its power in the desiring,
nothing but deception in the satisfaction. The freshness of
virgin passion is but a fleeting impression, a felicity progressively corroded by mounting experience. This precarious transport and its irrevocable dissolution with time is the source of
the young lover's sadness. The moment of meditation is a
flash of universal experience, in which the youth regrets the
elusive ideal in all human desire.

Certainly he who is deaf to the promptings of the celestial
voices may indulge his sensual urge in the kind of epicurean
retreat from life's adversities and frustrations suggested by
the poem "Italie":

> Pour échapper aux maux que fait la destinée,
> Pour jouir ici-bas des fleurs de ma saison,
> Et doucement couler cette humaine journée,
> Que me faut-il? . . . du ciel, de l'onde et du gazon,
>
> Et, quand pâlit au soir la lumière affaiblie,
> Une amoureuse voix, qui meurt à mon côté,

Qui dit *non* bien souvent et bien souvent l'oublie,
Des pleurs dans deux beaux yeux, un beau sein agité.

Although the compensatory joys of the flesh provide a practical means of self-oblivion, there is no suggestion in this poem of any fidelity in the erotic experience. Nor does the carnal enjoyment of the prostitute in the poem "Rose" inspire any honorable emotion:

Aux soupirs de l'alcôve, on dirait de l'amour.
Mais, hélas! quand parmi ces fureurs de jeunesse
Tarit la jouissance, . . . avant qu'elle renaisse, . . .
Même aux bras l'un de l'autre, oh! que l'amour est loin!

Amidst the increasing desolation of the advancing years, there is a desperate confusion between carnal passion and the "volupté" of the spirit. The sonnet "Des laves du Vésuve une goutte enflammée" expresses the despairing lover's desire to find eternal felicity in the ecstasy of one voluptuous hour of autumnal love:

Oh! qu'à ce sein je puisse, avant mon soir aussi,
Mieux qu'antique camée ou lave au flot durci,
Clouer mon front brûlant, toute une heure . . . éternelle!

But the transports of physical passion are ultimately halted by a feeling of distaste, which begins a downward movement of deprivation and negation. From this relapse springs a new tone in the Delorme poems, compounded of timidity, hesitancy, sentimental consolation, bantering irony, and cloying nostalgia, which becomes characteristic of the *élégie analytique* specified by Baudelaire in his letter of January, 1866.[6]

The descending curve of eroticism in Delorme is psychologically more interesting than the ascending development of idealism, for it produces an effusion of sentiment in half-tones,

6. Baudelaire, *Correspondance générale*, V, 218.

which makes a striking contrast with the sonorous full-blooded expression of the first-generation Romantics. There comes a stage in the hero's psychological history (reflected to some extent by Sainte-Beuve himself in 1838) in which the promises of first love and promiscuity alike have failed. The frustrated poet is driven to new terrain to seek compensation and consolation. His role henceforth will be that of a successor and consoler, forming new liaisons in which both participants accept something less than the attainment of the first lofty ideals. The full ardor has gone out of love, which is now a fragile emotion of compromise, reservation, restriction. This compromise, enforced by destiny, now becomes the essence of plaint in the elegy. Bruised and anemic hearts seek out each other in order to preserve, under the menace of approaching extinction in death, what measure of serenity and emotional security can be saved from the debacle of life. In fresh arrangements of love can be found new hopes, but there must be modesty of ambition. So, in the sonnet "Oh! laissez-vous aimer! . . . ce n'est pas un retour," the lover seeks only the subtle delight of a cerebral intimacy:

> Ce n'est pas d'enlacer en mes bras le contour
> De ces bras, de ce sein; d'embraser de ma flamme
> Ces lèvres de corail si fraîches; non, madame,
> Mon feu pour vous est pur, aussi pur que le jour.

> Mais seulement, le soir, vous parler à la fête,
> Et tout bas, bien longtemps, vers vous penchant la tête,
> Murmurer de ces riens qui vous savent charmer;

This modest dream is misinterpreted by the loved one, so that the poet, with gracious stoicism, abandons his hope and accepts the finality of his emotional wretchedness. In different circumstances, such as those related in "Causerie au bal," there will perhaps be the hope of resuming a previously tempestuous relationship on new terms of serene affection:

Et je vous ai revue, et d'espérance avide
J'ai rougi; près de vous un fauteuil était vide;
Et votre œil sans courroux sur moi s'est reposé,
Et je me suis assis, et nous avons causé:

But woe unto the suitor who, by too bold a move, seeks in small presumptions to revive a past closed for ever. If only to preserve the nostalgia of desultory conversation, he is well advised not to reopen the old wounds of love or regret.

The propitious circumstances have to be found in which, bridging the tempestuous years between adolescence and maturity, two afflicted souls may seek solace in a new happiness together. In the poem "La contredanse" Delorme uses the metaphor of two torrents, which, when the turbulence of early passion subsides, discover each other and flow as two calm springs into a lake of harmony. The meeting of kindred hearts seeking tardy consolation for the deceptions of life's promises is further defined in the poem "Après une lecture d'Adolphe." Why should not the disillusioned twenty-year-old dream of a consoling relationship with some equally disconsolate widow? On her isolated country estate, they would pass their time in the subtly nostalgic analysis of sentimental novels or in the delicious languor of an autumnal affection. A similar pattern of consolation is developed in the composition dedicated "A Madame *** qui avait lu avec attendrissement les poésies d'un jeune auteur qu'elle croyait mort." Here the compassionate patroness would restore some measure of youthful enthusiasm to the young poet buried alive in a grave of bitter isolation from the world. Hearts wounded in their earliest encounters with love must grasp the propitious moment of consolation before the lacerations deteriorate into the gangrene of spiritual disintegration and remorse. To mitigate the pain of old age and dying, they feel a deep need for the kind of affectionate companionship expressed in the poem "Amie, il faut aimer quand le feu couve encore":

> Amie, il faut aimer pour qu'à l'heure où tout passe,
> A l'âge où toutes fleurs quitteront le chemin,
> Dans les landes du soir, en entrant, tête basse,
> Nous nous serrions la main.

Delorme's tendency toward calmer and more discreet amatory adventures imposes an almost disciplined austerity upon his courtship: for example, the decorous stratagem of the sonnet "Une soirée encore était presque passée" and the circumspect pathos of the verses "Pour mon cher Marmier: sur l'Elster." From encounter to encounter the player in the game of love has become wiser. Love at first lured youth like a calm sea with the promise of supreme bliss, but its subsequent storms led him to seek serenity far from the turbulent brilliance of the ocean, in "les bois, et l'ombre, et les gazons." In the light of experience, Eros is found assuming various ironic personalities: the agent of the law of retaliation in "Traduit de Moschus, II"; the whimsical trickster of the poem "Pour mon ami Auguste Desplaces"; or the artful contriver in "Traduit de Moschus, III."

The elements of compensation and consolation in the autumn season of love represent for Delorme a diminution of the original ideal felicity. They are the only fruits of a search for what Baudelaire later called the "extase de la vie."[7] The frustrations and imperfections encountered by Delorme in his pursuit of earthly happiness focus attention on the other pole of the hero's spiritual duality. The disciple Baudelaire again furnished a definition when he named this other pole the "horreur de la vie."[8] This negative postulation of the spirit embraces a disgust with the experiences of this world prompted by the mysterious attraction of the transcendental—the dream

7. Baudelaire, "Mon cœur mis à nu," *Œuvres complètes*, II, 758.
8. *Ibid.*

[28]

of "saintes voluptés"[9]—and a yearning for penetration of the metaphysical mysteries. Like other artists, the poet is particularly susceptible to the messages of celestial voices. The projection of his spirit beyond this world nullifies mundane values for Joseph Delorme and brings about his ennui, the most striking symptom of the Romantic *mal du siècle,* as well as the basic constituent of modern anguish.

The physical portrait of the hero in "En m'en revenant un soir d'été" provides an effective introduction to the biography of ennui in Delorme's poems. It is the picture of a body prematurely aged by life's physical adversities and of an anguished soul floundering hopelessly amidst the *horreur de la vie:*

Que faudrait-il, hélas! pour que cette grande âme
Reprît goût à la vie et ranimât sa flamme?
Jeune, comme il vieillit! comme il se traîne seul!
A le voir si voûté, l'on dirait un aïeul!
Il se ride, il jaunit, il penche vers la tombe;
Du front, chaque matin, une mèche lui tombe;
Sans doute, bien des coups, dès longtemps, l'ont blessé;
Son destin finira, tel qu'il a commencé,
Dans l'ennui, dans les pleurs; il connaît trop la vie,
Et combien tout est vain dans tout ce qu'on envie;
Sans doute, il sait trop bien ce que valent de soins,
La gloire, le bonheur,—fantôme!—Mais, au moins,
Si quelque chose ici le consolait encore!
Car son génie ardent, chaque nuit, se dévore,
Comme la lampe, au soir, laissée en un caveau,
Sans qu'une vierge y verse un aliment nouveau.

This final abject state is, however, but the termination of a gradual spiritual disintegration. In "L'enfant rêveur" the ideal-

___

9. Massin, *Baudelaire "entre Dieu et Satan,"* p. 44. The expression "saintes voluptés" in Baudelaire's poem "Bénédiction" is here interpreted as a quasi-religious ecstasy.

ism of the dreamer is confronted only too early with the cruel horror of human existence:

> Pauvre enfant qui plongeais avec une foi d'ange,
> Qu'à ton œil détrompé soudainement tout change!
> Au lieu des blancs cristaux, des bosquets de corail,
> Des nymphes aux yeux verts assises en sérail
> Et tressant sous leurs doigts, à défaut de feuillages,
> Les solides rameaux semés de coquillages,
> Qu'as-tu vu sous les eaux! précipices sans fond,
> Arêtes de rocher, sable mouvant qui fond,
> Monstres de toute forme entrelacés en groupe,
> Serpents des mers, dragons à tortueuse croupe,
> Crocodiles vomis du rivage africain,
> Et plus affreux de tous, le vorace requin.

Yet in the unfolding experience of life, youth, in spite of frustration and disappointment, is seldom completely deprived of happiness. Real ennui begins only when the novelty of life's phenomena is exhausted, when an awakened taste for living is stifled in a subsequent inertia of will and spirit. Before that happens, the victim is affected intermittently by several different aspects of spleen.

In "Le soir de la jeunesse," Delorme congratulates a friend who by calm philosophy has triumphed over the spiritual tyranny imposed by the transports of erotic passion. But he counsels vigilance against the danger of a relapse following such a victory. There are times when the philosopher can drift into a condition of ennui in which the mind's energy and the heart's newly won tranquillity are devoured by an aimless and futile emotionalism founded on a disappointed early love.

Another special state of spleen derives from complete separation from the normal affections and sentiments of human society—absence of family ties or the bonds of warm friendship. This condition produces in "La veillée" a particularly heavy atmosphere of gloom. The macabre scene terminating the poem, reflecting intense emotional and spiritual aridity, has a remarkably flat tone:

> Mais rien; nul effroi saint; pas de souvenir tendre;
> Je regarde sans voir, j'écoute sans entendre,
> Chaque heure sonne lente, et lorsque, par trop las
> De ce calme abattant et de ces rêves plats,
> Pour respirer un peu je vais à la fenêtre
> (Car au ciel de minuit le croissant vient de naître),
> Voilà soudain, qu'au toit lointain d'une maison,
> Non pas vers l'orient, s'embrase l'horizon,
> Et j'entends résonner, pour toute mélodie,
> Des aboiements de chiens hurlant dans l'incendie.

The psychological desolation of "La veillée" finds a parallel in the physical dullness of the rural landscape in "La plaine." The atmosphere in this poem is one of deprivation, decay, want, exhaustion, and poverty—a complete negation of fruitfulness. The landscape is peopled only by those drawn there by life's harsh necessities, and its mournful atmosphere attracts an answering gloom in the mood of the poet surveying the scene:

> Mais dans la plaine, quoi? des jachères pierreuses,
> Et de maigres sillons en veines malheureuses,
> Que la bêche, à défaut de charrue, a creusés;
> Et sur des ceps flétris des échalas brisés;
> De la cendre par place, un reste de fumée,
> Et le sol tout noirci de paille consumée;
>
> . . . .
>
> D'ailleurs personne là pour son plaisir, sinon
> Des chasseurs, par les champs, regagnant leurs demeures,
> Sans avoir aperçu gibier depuis six heures . . .
> Moi pourtant je traverse encore à pas oisifs
> Et je m'en vais là-bas m'asseoir où sont les ifs.

The condition of solitude which produced the depressing tone of "La veillée" and "La plaine" has other manifestations in different contexts. It may, for example, be a desirable state, a coveted suspension of time's importunate course in which sensuous fantasies can be indulged. It appears in this form in "Au loisir." Solitude in the Delorme poems occurs more often, however, as an adverse circumstance of destiny, which either moves the poet to revolt or is accepted by him with an almost virtuous stoicism. Thus, in "Rayons jaunes," fate has imposed an absence of the joys of normal human affection in family ties. The feeling of isolation from the normal human experience drives Delorme to seek anonymous consolation in the life of the crowd, which, however, may ironically create a new source of spleen—the consciousness of the common man's moral ugliness. A similar rejection of society appears in the sonnet imitated from Wordsworth—"Je ne suis pas de ceux pour qui les causeries." Here it is the mediocrity of the provincial bourgeoisie which causes the poet to prefer a kind of mental and spiritual wilderness, whose only positive feature is a silence broken by the lugubrious sounds of the winter season. Ultimately Delorme sees in suicide the only logical issue from the impasse created by his rejection of the conditions of life. Yet his intention is devoid of hate, fearless and calmly reasoned. In "Le creux de la vallée," he envisages a stoic death in privacy as a fitting conclusion to a life of lonely suffering:

> J'ai toujours été seul à pleurer, à souffrir;
> Sans un cœur près du mien j'ai passé sur la terre;
> Ainsi que j'ai vécu, mourons avec mystère,
> Sans fracas, sans clameurs, sans voisins assemblés.

The physical solitude of nature is here once again paralleled with the psychological isolation of spleen.

The anxiety produced by the effect of time on man's life is an important factor contributing to Delorme's feeling of ennui.

[32]

In the poems of Joseph Delorme, as generally in French elegiac poetry of the Romantic period, the time theme centers upon two phenomena in the psychological and physical existence of every mortal: first, the curve rising from birth through adolescence into the flower of manhood, and finally falling in the decline of old age to ultimate and irrevocable death; second, the endless repetition of nature's cycle of seasons in opposition to the limited duration of any individual mortal span of life. These two cycles contain the possibility of numerous combinations of irony and contrast deriving from the exorbitant compass of man's desires compared with his relatively narrow restriction in time, space, and opportunity. The wave of ascent and decline in man's life is complicated by the fact that individual lives do not blossom, mature, and decline in unison. This circumstance creates a special irony in the contrast between contemporaneous but unequally developed physical and mental lives. The effect of duration on the human body and its faculties is obviously partly physical, but its poetic significance lies in the subjective impression created and active within the individual psyche. The anguish inherent in the consciousness of time is part of the philosophical tragedy of man's alternation between his spiritual and physical natures.

The rise and fall of Delorme's life regulated by time are presented in the sonnet "J'étais un arbre en fleur où chantait ma Jeunesse" through the metaphor of a tree visited by birds personifying youth and death:

Jeunesse, oiseau charmant, mais trop vite envolé,
Et même, avant de fuir du bel arbre effeuillé,
Il avait tant chanté qu'il se plaignait sans cesse.

. . . .

Tout se tait, tout est mort! L'arbre, veuf de chansons,
Étend ses rameaux nus sous les mornes saisons;
Quelque craquement sourd s'entend par intervalle;

[33]

Debout il se dévore, il se ride, il attend,
Jusqu'à l'heure où viendra la Corneille fatale
Pour le suprême hiver chanter le dernier chant.

The gap between the two limits of life's curve is emphasized in "Le dernier vœu," in which the normal erosion of advancing years is aggravated by a mortal affliction. The existence of the moribund poet is compared to that of an oak, which, with its bare trunk and blackened branches, is unworthy of embracing the delicately festooned vine. In "Le dernier vœu," the hero, saddened by his premature decline, seeks solace in observing the infectious happiness of youth, narrowing for a moment the distance between the two extremes of life's course. To the average mortal, the passing of the years brings an ample measure of adversity, of disappointment and shattered illusions, of sorrow in intimate personal tragedy. The gradual process of such an erosion for Delorme over a ten-year period is amply described in "La contredanse":

Dix ans, oh! n'est-ce pas? c'est bien long dans la vie,
Et c'est aussi bien court; les faux biens qu'on envie,
Tant de maux qu'on ignore, et les rêves déçus,
Doux essaims envolés aussitôt qu'aperçus;
Des êtres adorés que la tombe dévore;
Baiser deux yeux mourants et de ses mains les clore;
Dans un âpre sentier marcher sans avenir,
Monter, toujours monter, et ne voir rien venir;
Aimer sans espérance, ou brûler et se fondre
A se sentir aimer, et ne pouvoir répondre;
Souvent un pain amer, souvent la Pauvreté,
Au milieu d'un banquet où l'on n'est qu'invité,
Près de nous dans l'éclat s'asseyant comme une ombre;

The passing of time contributes notably to man's frustration because the moment lost is an irretrievable opportunity. Such moments may be those of potential self-fulfillment in a sober life of virtue, as in the poem "Toujours je la connus pensive et sérieuse." Or in another context the moment of time may mark a psychological peak, a moment of emotional fulfillment in the purity and clarity of adolescent love, as in the verses "A Alfred de Musset."

The special irony of time's flow is that mortals tend to behave as if there were no ravage, no physical change in the person, with its attendant effects upon the psychology of the ego. The inevitability of human decrepitude is common experience but cannot be accepted by the individual mind, whose conceits appear founded on the permanence of youthful freshness and beauty. In the poem "Rose," the courtesan is exhorted to contemplate a future whose cruel irrevocability brings tears to her eyes. Neither her floating fair tresses nor her pearl-white shoulder will last forever. The tumult of her lovers' adoration will subside into the silence of abandon, because physical charm will fade with the years. The similar decline of a popular actress' beauty forms the painful irony of "La suivante d'Emma." Her early admirers come in due course only to enjoy the brilliance of her conversation or to pay tribute to a monument of the past; but their eyes now are for the fresh charms of her young maid. A final commentary on human reluctance to accept the eventual consequences of time's erosion is offered in the poem "Le plus long jour de l'année," imitated from Wordsworth. Here nature's vernal renewal instils in the subjective consciousness a false security which makes the irony of physical decadence the more poignant. For mortals it is folly to let either the "frais ombrage" or the "fruits d'or dans le feuillage" of summer veil the gloomy future. The joys of life in its prime offer no solid foundation to meet the gravity of the eternal reckoning; faith in ephemeral beauty must yield to the more severe counsels of duty and virtue.

Despite the final ravage of time upon human yearning, the

autumnal season of love offers a temporary respite from this particular aspect of the *horreur de la vie*. Five of Delorme's poems embrace the theme of man's decline gracefully accepted in the twilight of life. In "Pensée d'automne" the poet sees the autumn brilliance as the reflection of spring's freshness and of high summer's splendors. This season in nature's cycle is transposed onto the psychology of man's declining years at the moment when the heart glances back upon the dreams and ardors of youth, as if in the secret hope of being born anew. This hope is especially cherished, for, unlike the regular rhythm of nature, the winter of life harbors the mystery of eternity. "Espérance" describes a lucidity of the soul which precedes the physical extinction of the mortal life. This prior enlightenment is welcomed as a pale reflection of the spiritual resurrection in the life beyond the grave. In the autumn of life the declining beauty of the loved one assumes an especially attractive sweetness, which is described in "Sous les derniers soleils de l'automne avancée":

> C'est la rose mourante et toujours plus touffue!
> Plus désirée à l'œil, la pêche qui va choir;
> La prune qui se fend et sa chair entrevue,
> Ivresse de l'abeille à son butin du soir!

In the poem "Imité d'Ovide," the poet, who has always valued love above all other divine gifts, craves in his declining years even the autumnal shadow of his earlier passion. The rebirth of nature in the spring is a cruel delight, for the old tender wounds of the heart are quick to reopen when memories are reawakened. Yet, before the awesome mystery of death, he craves a last drink at the chalice of erotic experience. From a different aspect, the twilight of life can offer a special security in love for those lonely hearts which make purposeful provision for the inevitable declining years:

Amie, il faut aimer pour qu'à l'heure où tout passe,
A l'âge où toutes fleurs quitteront le chemin,
Dans les landes du soir, en entrant, tête basse,
    Nous nous serrions la main.

All compensations duly considered, the relation of time and human life remains essentially a tragic one. It is symbolized in "Élégie" by the ephemeral sea of activity in man, whose ambition is unbounded, but whose nature is finite. All men—with their varied hopes, dreams, and plans—are equalized in their mortality like the restless waves of the ocean:

Mais toutes, aux mouvants, aux fragiles sommets,
A la marche plus humble, ou plus haut élancée,
Au plus ou moins d'éclat ou d'écume insensée,
Toutes, après leur bruit et leur feu d'un moment,
Au tournant du grand Cap, mouraient également!

Delorme's inability to accept the horrors of the purely earthly life is strongly influenced by the promptings of supernatural voices. They speak to him primarily as a poet, and it is as the anguish of the artist that the spiritual tragedy of Sainte-Beuve's hero assumes its most acute form. The comprehension of the universal analogy and the penetration of the transcendental mysteries achieved through poetry become the most frequent forms of escape for the hypersensitive soul oppressed by the evil of the world. Poetic expression becomes the only release of a genius yearning for a return to the unity of the Ideal. Agonizingly conscious of the disharmony between himself and his society, the artist-genius heeds the celestial voices and, by his heroic voyage into the unknown of the ethereal spheres, he offers himself as a sacrifice, through the spiritual tortures inherent in penetrating the awesome secrets of the supernatural. This sacrificial role of the poet appears later as an important theme in the poetry and poetic theory of Baudelaire, who develops it under the influence of Joseph de Maistre's doctrine of reversibility.[10]

As a chosen creature of God, the poet-child of "L'enfant rêveur" mourns his separation from his divine domicile. Reborn into a mortal incarnation of corruption, he is receptive at a very early age to the promptings of heavenly voices. His soul is seared by an endless longing for the Infinite from which he has been temporarily exiled. In the limpid innocence of childhood, the visions of a spirit still close to its celestial abode remain pure, but with adolescence and manhood comes a fusion of the Ideal with the tempting illusions of worldly materialism and concupiscence. The treacherous waters of the false *extase de la vie* claim their naïve prey:

> D'abord ce ne seront que vagues mélodies
> Dans les joncs, par degrés quelques voix plus hardies;
> Mais un jour te viendra l'âge d'homme, et pour lors
> Tu verras en ces eaux naître et fuir de beaux corps;
> Et tu voudras nager, et bien loin les poursuivre.
> On te dira des mots dont tout le cœur s'enivre,
> Et tu répondras *oui*.—Brûlant, plein de rougeur,
> De son rocher déjà s'est lancé le plongeur,
> Et l'onde refermée a blanchi sur sa tête,
> Comme un gouffre qui prend et garde sa conquête;

If the youthful victim should miraculously escape the torments of earthly deceptions, recovering enough courage to sing of his sufferings, the profane world would not comprehend the substance of his lament—the disharmony between the Ideal and the corruption of mortal existence. Perhaps by a belated miracle those who had suffered would come to appreciate such poetry, but this appreciation would do nothing to alleviate the essential anguish of its creator, torn as he is between the false

10. Daniel Vouga, *Baudelaire et Joseph de Maistre* (Paris: José Corti, 1957), pp. 51-60.

[38]

ecstasy of worldly temptations and the consciousness of the inadequacy of human existence.

The transcendental flight of intuitive dream in adolescent poetic genius produces its own special hazard. In the poem "Rêverie" the soul is represented as a still lake that reflects the heavens in their beauty and mystery. In the enjoyment of privileged perception of the heavenly mysteries, the artist aspires at his own peril to complete knowledge of the unity of the Ideal. Man, even the poet, cannot become divine. The mad hope of such a fusion of mortal in immortal can cause only chaos in the human soul:

> Amoureux de la grande image,
> D'abord j'en jouis à loisir;
> Bientôt désirant davantage,
> Poète avide, enfant peu sage,
> J'étends la main pour la saisir.

> Adieu soudain voûte étoilée,
> Blanche lumière, éclat si pur!
> Au sein de mon âme ébranlée,
> Phébé tremblante s'est voilée;
> L'image a perdu son azur.

The poetic soul will find fulfillment in the contemplation of only such divine secrets as are providentially revealed to it, in its function as interpreter to the vulgar of the symbols of the universal analogy.

In the chaotic struggle of his early manhood, Sainte-Beuve's hero turns to poetry for temporary comfort and tranquillity. It is, however, a wild and desolate terrain, very different from the charming strand of poetic reverie enjoyed by Lamartine in the Bay of Baïa.[11] Delorme's lyre is inspired rather on the stormy shore, where, in his "Adieux à la Poésie," the bittersweet of tempest and sunshine would match his spleen:

11. Alphonse de Lamartine, *Méditations poétiques*, ed. Paul Vernière (Paris: Delmas, 1949), pp. 120-123.

Mais, au lieu d'une tiède brise,
Des vents l'orageuse rumeur
Bat des rochers à tête grise,
Et de la vague qui se brise
Gémit l'éternelle clameur.

Sur une grève désolée,
Pour tromper mes ennuis amers,
Tout le jour, ma lyre exilée
Répétait sa plainte mêlée
Au bruit monotone des mers.

Yet there is no permanent solace in poetry. Eventually the hero obeys the call to re-engagement in the stream of life. In the light of gathering frustration and disillusion, this elected course may well come to lack any logical objective, unless it be the relief of life's tedium in the final oblivion of death. Ironically, the remembered joys of poetry provide refreshment and repose for the soul exhausted in this perpetual and purposeless marathon.

In "Retour à la Poésie" Delorme's election of engagement is shown to have been vain. Yet he has paid a small price for some invaluable truths about himself. This incomplete genius has felt the agonizing struggle between his own spiritual constitution and the profane world of men. Even as he sat at the sensuous banquet of life, he saw like King Belshazzar the indelible writing on the wall which confirmed his own personal dilemma. His soul could not disclaim its function as the mirror of the divine, yet it could no more fuse with the Absolute than it could accept the false *extase de la vie* offered in the earthly existence. Chosen genius must receive the call of the Infinite as Hamlet heeded the summons of his father's ghost, a summons both loved and feared. But the special understanding which falls to the poet's intuitive perception implies a special burden of spiritual torment, which is interpreted by the vulgar, as in the case of Shakespeare's prince, only as madness. The destiny of the artist-genius thus must be a heavy sacrifice of his worldly personality because of his increasing preoccupation with the music of the "harpe secrète" and with the introspection of his own soul, which reflects the splendors of the Infinite.

To illustrate his conception of the poet's sacrificial role, Delorme uses two special examples of artistic single-mindedness. In the verses "A mon ami Victor Hugo," the fickle esteem of common men changes from rejection to adulation of the great poet. The true genius, however, completely engulfed in his upward surge to the celestial regions of the Infinite, remains unconcerned by the approval or disapproval of the uninitiate:

> Ou bien, sans rien sentir de ce vain bruit qui passe,
> Plein des accords divins, le regard dans l'espace
> Fixé sur un soleil,
> Plonges-tu, pour l'atteindre, en des flots de lumière,
> Et bientôt, t'y posant, laisses-tu ta paupière
> S'y fermer au sommeil?

The poet's sacrifice is enhanced to the status of martyrdom in "Le cénacle," which becomes almost a battle hymn composed for a select band of Romantic poets, including Hugo, Vigny, Lamartine, and—by association in the fraternity of the arts—the painter Boulanger. Following the example of the disciples of early Christianity, these elect few must brave the disdainful opposition of society and carry the banner of poetic truth fearlessly on to a victory which will reconcile the masses:

> Tous réunis, s'entendre, et s'aimer, et se dire:
> Ne désespérons point, poètes, de la lyre,
> Car le siècle est à nous.
> Il est à vous; chantez, ô voix harmonieuses,
> Et des humains bientôt les foules envieuses
> Tomberont à genoux.

Certain hazards attendant upon the creation and publication of any literary work contribute to the spasmodic splenetic moods of the poet. In the poem, "Pour un ami—La veille de la publication d'un premier ouvrage," it is a question of the choice between the tranquillity of obscure melancholy and a stormy progress toward artistic recognition. In retrospect the successful artist wonders whether the clamor of renown is as precious as the freedom of secluded reverie. In his novitiate the trials and errors of his creative imagination could be executed without public notice and his natural talent exercised without strain. Thereafter, the modesty of the novice gives way to the tyranny of the search for public acclaim, and this growing ambition spells diminishing tranquillity:

> Mais, depuis, l'orgueil en délire
> A pris mon cœur comme un tyran;
> Je ne sais plus à quoi j'aspire;
> Ma nacelle est un grand navire,
> Et me voilà sur l'Océan.

Another source of ennui for Delorme is the exhaustion of artistic inspiration. In "Le calme," the hero is poised like a ship before a tremendous adventure in poetic sublimation. Yet there is no immediate flow of creative energy. The vessel is becalmed and must await a fair wind:

> Adieu, rivage, adieu!—Mais la mer est dormante,
> Plus dormante qu'un lac; mieux vaudrait la tourmente;
> Mais d'en-haut, ce jour-là, nul souffle ne répond;
> La voile pend au mât et traîne sur le pont.

The strain of composition is increased by the narrow choice of lyric genres imposed on the poet by his particular position in the Romantic movement. Compared with her sisters in French Romanticism, the frail and humble heroine of Delorme's "Ma muse" is poorly endowed; yet she is able, given the best conditions, to extract the very essence of poetry from banal and lugubrious subjects. Moreover, she holds the key to the comprehension of the universal analogy and to the grasp of infinite truth:

Vierge, relève un peu ce long crêpe de veuve;
Oublie un peu tes maux; que ta parole pleuve
Goutte à goutte, plaintive, à mon cœur enflammé
Aussi fraîche qu'aux fleurs est la rosée en mai;
Et pâle, dénouant ta chevelure brune,
Redeviens belle encore aux rayons de la lune.
O Muse, alors dis-moi, Muse chère à jamais,
Les noms mystérieux des âmes que j'aimais;
Puis porte mes regards à la céleste toile,
Et par leurs noms aussi nomme-moi chaque étoile, . . .

The poet sees in those supernatural powers of the muse the promise of a better world to come after mortal life. Such is the reward due to the elect soul which has sacrificed itself for the benefit of humanity:

Surtout dis-moi qu'il est là-haut un meilleur monde,
Où pour les cœurs choisis un saint bonheur abonde.

*   *   *

From the haphazardly compiled collection of the Delorme poems, certain categories of psychological experience emerge, which together form the whole climate of anguish in this particular *malade du siècle*. The disorder of composition makes it highly unlikely that Sainte-Beuve intended for this work any formal unity tantamount to a definite aesthetic of anguish. It rather appears that he was merely conscious of expressing certain sentiments or moods which, while related to his personal life, were also characteristic of the young Romantic of his era. Analysis does, in fact, reveal a basic psychological pattern capable of standing as an aesthetic of the *mal du siècle*. This pattern explains Delorme's Romantic agony in terms of the simultaneous postulation of his soul toward the finite and the infinite, with a dual polarity existing between the *extase de la vie* and the *horreur de la vie*. The rising curve of felicity which depends upon the attraction of the *extase* is countered by a decline of disenchantment activated by the ravages of the *horreur*. Torn between the counter-attractions of the finite world and the transcendental Ideal, the spirit falls into a state of inertia. From this paralysis of the soul there are only two apparent issues. First, there is in the present, finite life an intimation, through poetic creation, of the eternal paradise of the Absolute. This is achieved, for an elect band of divinely inspired artists, by the apprehension of the universal analogy in the poetic transformation of the finite world. Second, in the absence of artistic creation, there is in physical death a release of the spirit to a better life beyond the grave.

The disciple Baudelaire proclaimed his admiration for specific compositions in the *Poésies de Joseph Delorme*. His letter to Sainte-Beuve of January 25, 1862, mentioned the "Rayons jaunes." That of January 15, 1866, cited "La veillée," "Le creux de la vallée," "Rose," "La plaine," and the "Stances, poème imité de Kirke White." The tone of all these poems is that of deep melancholy, and in at least three—"La veillée," "Le creux de la vallée," and "La plaine"—there is a particularly acrid savor of spleen. The adolescent Baudelaire, at a stage in his poetic formation summarized by Marcel Ruff under the heading "Le titre pétard,"[12] was likely to be impressed by such poems. By March, 1865, certainly, the disciple was hailing the Delorme collection as the *"Fleurs du Mal* de la veille." This appreciation, it should be noted, was made four years after the 1861 edition of Baudelaire's own poems, in which the disciplinary effect of psychological unity on the composition and

12. Ruff, *L'esprit du mal*, p. 230.

sequence of the *Fleurs* was abundantly clear. The younger poet thus showed himself willing to extend to obviously paler and less exquisite flowers the deeply significant title and the dominating aesthetic of his own masterpiece. It is improbable that, in 1844, when Baudelaire addressed to Sainte-Beuve his verses in praise of Delorme and Amaury, the disciple's sensitive genius would have missed the psychological import of Delorme's lyricism. He surely would have recognized that these poems viewed as a whole represented an itinerary of the spirit in Romantic ennui. The painful themes of the many poems which Baudelaire had already composed by 1844 indicated that, in the developing tragedy of his personal life, he found Delorme's itinerary quite close to his own. It is, therefore, scarcely surprising that only four years later, in 1848, the young poet should furnish an aesthetic program for his first published group of poems. His *Limbes* were then announced as a portrayal of the anguish of his generation. The real significance of his praise of Sainte-Beuve in 1844 is that he applied Delorme's vague pattern of human duality to the circumstances of his own spiritual pilgrimage in the *Fleurs du Mal*. In the *Poésies de Joseph Delorme* the conception of the double postulation in the hero's soul carried but shallow religious emphasis. Only the conscious religiosity of the *Consolations* and *Volupté* offered later a specifically Christian solution to the anguish created by the *horreur de la vie*. In contrast, the *Fleurs du Mal* evidences a grave theological preoccupation with the function of evil in modern spleen.

The true poetic legacy of Sainte-Beuve is to be measured in the dimensions of moral psychology. The *mal du siècle*, as demonstrated in the spiritual and moral duality of Delorme, was absorbed by Baudelaire and translated by him in the personal idiom of his own vital experience. The process of translation, conducted over a period of some twenty years, will be examined in a subsequent chapter.

3. Les Consolations—*A temporary religious solution to Delorme's moral dilemma*

The largely psychological exposition of spiritual duality effected by the critical intelligence in the Delorme poems undergoes a transformation in the *Consolations*. In this second collection of Sainte-Beuve's poems, the alternatives of the moral dilemma are redefined in specifically religious terms, whereby the sublime is synonymous with the Christian deity and the profane is identified with the antithesis, evil. Although Baudelaire came only gradually to appreciate the religiosity of the *Consolations*, it is significant that he admitted to a better understanding of these poems by 1866, by which time he was thoroughly dismayed by the theological gravity of his own spiritual catastrophe. Moreover, to the younger poet, all of Sainte-Beuve's poetry published by 1830 appeared principally as a preparation for the novel *Volupté*. The Christian explanation of the *vie insuffisante* discerned by Delorme's moral lucidity is important as an introduction to the more complex theology that informs Amaury's confession and suggests the issue from his spiritual disaster. Notwithstanding Baudelaire's lack of enthusiasm for the *Consolations*, it is clear that this work, together with *Volupté*, forms the basis for Thibaudet's formula of *christianisme intérieur* in Sainte-Beuve's lyrical production.

While not strictly relevant to Delorme's particular crisis, some verses located at the end of chapter xxi in *Volupté* were considered by Sainte-Beuve sufficiently in the general tone of the *Consolations* for them to be annexed to this collection. Where certain of Amaury's experiences contribute to the examination of religiosity in the present chapter, some quotations are made as if from a true *Consolation*.

Upon dedicating his second collection of poetry to Victor Hugo in December, 1829, Sainte-Beuve admitted a serious need of some solution to the spiritual and moral chaos of Joseph Delorme. In the preceding chapter this disorder was assessed in terms of the bipolarity in man's soul, which causes an alternation between the sublime and the profane in mortal experience. With no taste for life and no hope of immortality, Delorme falls into despair; his final habitat in the *Poésies de Joseph Delorme* is a desert of spleen. In the preface to the *Consolations*, the despairing poet grasps the strength of the righteous and prophetic friend as the source of spiritual salvation. For Delorme it is a question first of renewing faith merely in the transitory life of man's world. The spiritual guide must first apply his efforts to giving back to the anguished wanderer a taste for living itself. Thereafter, this reawakened desire for meaningful participation in the human struggle will grow into a passion for eternal life and the assurance that it can be achieved. This final stage of the spiritual progress, whereby the soul is restored from disintegration to fulness of life, can be attained only through the discipline and the immutable forms of the Christian religion.

Conscious as he was of his spiritual needs, Sainte-Beuve did not aspire to the highest exaltation of his friend Hugo. Rather he was concerned with achieving the humbler consolations of an honest but unpretentious obscurity. He admitted only that, within this restricted framework, the *Consolations* were a faithful reflection of his spiritual state at a certain stage of his life.[1] The author insisted that in these poems he had not departed from the vulgar reality on which he had operated in the *Poésies de Joseph Delorme*. Immediate reality, translated through the Absolute, had merely yielded more sublime conclusions. Sainte-Beuve equated the moral progress herein implied with a superior poetic power.

The *Consolations* can be viewed as a recapitulation of the spiritual dilemma originally described in the "mal de Joseph Delorme," but in this collection of poems the dualism of the soul is stated in specifically Christian terms. The *extase de la vie* has become the aspiration toward God of a contrite Delorme. The *horreur de la vie* is now a condition of spiritual frustration caused by absence from God. Inherent in the *horreur* are the agonies of vices motivated by the essential ennui of separation from the divine. This separation is otherwise defined as sin. From the Christian perspective, the dual polarity of the human soul is seen as sin, or *horreur*, and divine beatitude, or *extase*. Many of the components of man's total psychological experience can be analyzed from one pole or the other. Thus such varying aspects of life as love, death, spleen, artistic genius, pride, and time can all be related to the concept of man's spiritual frustration; similarly, love, humility, peace, and poetic creation can be related to divine inspiration within the *extase* of spiritual fulfillment.

Love, viewed as a feature of the *horreur de la vie*, assumes a carnal nature and becomes, for the Christian, profane. The de-

1. The majority of the *Consolations* were written during the period August-December, 1829.

sires of the flesh and their satisfaction appear in the poem "A M. Viguier" as the aftermath of a fruitless search for absolute truth by the philosophers of pre-Christian Greece. Habitually youth rejects its early childhood nurture in the sacred word of God, seeking wisdom and peace in the delirium of sensual indulgence. The bitter awareness of the ultimate vanity of such a choice is illustrated in the verses "A M. A. de L[amartine]": "Bonheur vain! fol espoir! délire d'une fièvre!/ Coupe qu'on croyait fraîche et qui brûle la lèvre!"

From the Christian point of view, the most serious aspect of the sins of the flesh is that the individual sinner assumes responsibility for leaving his soul in danger of eternal damnation. For example, in the poem "A mon ami Leroux," the worship of the idol of sensuality is seen not only as an arrogant defiance of the divine, but also—more agonizing in itself—as a wanton sacrifice of the soul. Intoxicated by sensual pleasures, the spirit slowly becomes incapable of honorable passions.

At the pole of the *horreur de la vie*, death, like carnal love, is nothing but spiritual sterility. Instead of the promise of immortal life, there is substituted a senseless and bestial oblivion, "une mort sans réveil" or "une nuit sans jour," sought often by total engulfment in sensuality ("A mon ami Ulric Guttinguer"). But just as the soul in this life yearns for ideal love, so after its worldly exile it craves to blossom in the beatitude of reunion with the divine ("A Fontenay").

Because nothing but the Divine Absolute can satisfy the highest ardor of the human spirit, man's essential dissatisfaction with the profane produces a state of ennui, which he attempts to dissolve by resorting again to the profane distractions. The monotonous aimlessness of this condition—the natural result of separation from God—is described in the poem "A M. de L[amartine]." This same composition, in the words of Lamartine's own advice to the poet, offers a return to God as the only solution to the spiritual dilemma inseparable from the condition. The ennui inherent in separation from the divine paradise is illustrated in two other *Consolations*: in "A Alfred de Vigny" as a necessary feature of the artist's exile on earth; in "A mon ami Prosper Mérimée" as a renewal of hate through recurring political strife.

In examining, purely as phenomena in themselves, the pains and vexations inherent in the negative half of man's moral duality, one is led to reflect that many of them result from his feeling self-sufficient and superior. Pride, as in "A mon ami Victor Pavie," may choose as truth the mystical delirium of adolescent genius; whereas spiritual wisdom enjoins a humbler perseverance in the way of the Divine Shepherd. In the poem entitled "A mon ami Paul Lacroix. Les larmes de Racine," an over-confident spirit is misled into emphasizing the ostentation of praise rather than the humility of repentance. In the verses annexed from chapter xxi of *Volupté*, the tremor of pride under some unjust accusation is held inferior to a humble examination of the innermost recesses of one's own soul.

Within the destructive totality of the *horreur de la vie*, one of the most erosive functions is that exercised by time. The Christian tone of the *Consolations* suggests a contrast between the unstable human conception of time and the immutable unity of divine eternity. Such a contrast is indeed presented in the poem "A M. Auguste le Prévost," which is based upon the notion of oblivion. The dead can find little security in the short memories of the living. Permanent trust should rather be reposed by man in his Divine Creator, who is ever forgiving and never forgetful of His most precious creature. The action of time in changing the spiritual attitude of the individual and in steadily eroding the innocent purity of early years may be examined in the verses addressed "A Mademoiselle ——." With the passing of the years, the original pure image of the poet can no longer be recognized by the beloved companion of his childhood. It is now a question, for a soul corrupted by the temptations of the world, of rising to partake again of the "voluptés pures."

Poetic creation, a prominent theme in the anguish of Delorme and in the metaphysical dilemma depicted in Baudelaire's *Fleurs du Mal*, is presented in the religiously oriented *Consolations* as divine gifts of talent and inspiration. Through their use in his art, the poet bears witness to God as the unique source of all truth, goodness and beauty. Hence, the wasteful dissipation of those Heaven-sent gifts implies a blasphemous misdirection of the divine purposes in art. This abuse, as a separation from God, is a source of spiritual frustration for the artist, and becomes naturally an element in the *horreur de la vie*. The artist's obligation to the divine source of his genius and his failure to discharge the debt in his created works are among the themes of the poem "A M. Viguier."

The gift of poetic genius is often dissipated through defects or errors within the individual artist. For example, poetic ardor may wander along the deceptive paths of an immature fantasy during the poet's formative years, as may be seen in the poems "A M. Alphonse de Lamartine" and "A mon ami Victor Pavie." Artistic creation also carries for the poet frustrations which are outside his own control and are part of the climate of adversity in which he strives to realize his genius. Among other trials, he has always to endure the ridicule of the uninitiated masses ("Sonnet imité de Wordsworth," *Consolation* XV). The agonizing difficulty of poetic creation, when the source of divine inspiration is temporarily exhausted, drives the poet from celestial splendors back into terrestrial mediocrity. The ennui of poetic sterility tempts him to the banquet of profane pleasures. From this feast of horror, he is driven by the accusing summons of artistic conscience:

Il entre dans la fête et tout entier s'y livre,

. . . .

—Jusqu'à ce qu'une voix que n'entend point l'oreille,
Comme le chant du coq, à l'aube le réveille,
Ou que sur la muraille un mot divin tracé
Le chasse du festin, Balthazar insensé. ("A Boulanger")

The antithesis to the negative postulation of the poet's soul
—the *horreur de la vie*—is equated in the *Consolations* with a
life in the Christian deity. In this *extase de la vie*, the frustrations due to separation from God are changed into fulfillment
by the divine presence; man's sufferings are assuaged by the
comfort of God; and his desires are satisfied by His all-embrac-
ing love and perfect beauty. The repentant return of the
estranged heart to God forms the theme of the poem, "A mon
ami Prosper Mérimée":

Ainsi, plongé longtemps au plus bas de l'abîme,
Enfermé dans la fosse où je niais le Ciel,
Ainsi le repentir descendait sur mon crime,
Et je sortais vivant, pareil à Daniel!

. . . .

Cru mort de tous, pleuré de ma tribu chérie,
Ainsi l'ombre sortait un jour de mon chemin;
Dieu disait de couler à la source tarie;
Et j'embrassais encor Jacob et Benjamin!

But before the divine voice can be heard, the clamor of mortal
and profane pleasures must be stilled in a heart henceforth
vigilant against the temptations of the senses.

In contrast with the love of the flesh, the love which participates in the *extase de la vie* is spiritual and divinely ideal.
Within a specifically Christian framework, a markedly Platonic
tone is evident in the poem "A mon ami Ulric Guttinguer."
Two kindred souls united by a common faith in God triumph
over both life and death. This Platonic tone appears again in
the *Consolation* addressed "A mon ami Antony Deschamps,"
in which the author envies the fate of this poet who has found

inspiration for his art and for his life in the sublime love of a woman:

> Plus j'y reviens, et plus j'honore le poète,
> Qui, fixant, dès neuf ans, sa pensée inquiète,
> Eut sa Dame, et l'aima sans lui rien demander;
> La suivit comme on suit l'astre qui doit guider,
> S'en forma tout d'abord une idée éternelle,
> Et, quand la Mort la prit dans le vent de son aile,
> N'eut, pour se souvenir, qu'à regarder en lui;

In a different key, the essence of honest family life appears in the poem "A Ernest Fouinet" as mortal love—filial, conjugal, parental, fraternal—which is itself nurtured in the love of God and in the acceptance of His will for man.

Life in God, which is the religious foundation of the *extase de la vie* as presented in the *Consolations,* demands a basic personal humility. This humility is seen from various aspects: withdrawal from the ostentation of the world; straitened material circumstances; simple domestic felicity; the routine of commonplace duties monotonously fulfilled. Several examples of duty faithfully discharged or adversity bravely endured are offered in the poem "A Ernest Fouinet": the young girl who passes her days under the silent discipline of the convent; the young bride who, instead of setting up an independent household with her husband, raises her family under the wing of her parents; or the poor young student who is unable to travel or to give freedom to the normal transports of his heart.

Sainte-Beuve has shown that poetic creation is active, because of its pains and frustrations, in the negative field of man's spiritual bipolarity. However, he attaches greater importance to the positive activity of such creation, which can be a true *extase.* He sees the poetic art, in the *Consolations,* as an instrument of God designed to develop and enrich man's spiritual life; for the true poet interprets the divine unity through the symbols of the universal analogy. Of all the poems in this collection, that addressed "A mon ami Leroux" examines most extensively the divine qualities of art in general— "L'Art sublime, éternel et divin," which is radiant "comme la Vertu." In the course of this composition, Michelangelo is portrayed at the close of his life as fearful of erecting a false idol. In this fear he is deceived, for since art is divinely inspired, it inevitably leads the artist to God:

> Tous ces mortels choisis, qui, dans l'humanité,
> Réfléchissent le ciel par quelque grand côté,
> Iront-ils, au moment d'adorer face à face
> Le Soleil éternel devant qui tout s'efface,
> Appeler feu follet l'astre qui les conduit,
> Ou l'ardente colonne en marche dans leur nuit?

Because the Divine Being is the source and archetype of all beauty, art is but a reflection of that One, lovingly perceived by an elite band of mortals through the infinitely diverse symbolism of the universe. The inspired artist is a workman of God, building on earth a temple of divine truth and beauty. Pertinent to the construction of this edifice, the verses addressed "A Victor Hugo" refer to a sanctuary of "la sainte Poésie," whence the poet emerges as conqueror in a struggle of attrition between divine inspiration and the obstinate intractability of his material:

> Honneur à toi, Poète;—honneur à toi, vainqueur!
> Oh! garde-les toujours, jeune homme au chaste cœur,
> Garde-les sur ton front ces auréoles pures,
> Et ne les ternis point par d'humaines souillures.
> La sainte Poésie environne tes pas:
> C'est le plus bel amour des amours d'ici-bas.

Since art is divinely inspired, the true artist must possess humility in his vocation. For example, in the poem "A mon ami Boulanger" the association of artistic genius with the cult of earthly fame is regarded as an uneasy relationship. Conversely, the austere fate of those medieval cathedral architects who have long since passed into oblivion is entirely in keeping with the virtuous character of the Christian artist. Rather than a personal triumph, artistic creation is primarily a toil—the artist's faithful response to the expectations of the Master Creator. The Christian interpretation of poetic inspiration recognizes the apostolic role of the artist, giving particular emphasis to his share in the divine splendor, his sacrificial martyrdom, his intercession for souls in purgatory, his final resurrection into the bosom of God. In the poem "A Alfred de Vigny," the poet makes a sacrificial descent from the celestial realm, where he was sheltered from the antipathy of ordinary men. The artist, illuminating for the masses the transcendental and eternal divine mysteries, becomes through his work the consolation of souls who are in the purgatory of spiritual aridity. His mission completed, his just reward is to be raised again into permanent reunion with God.

The *Consolations* express many important aspects of the *extase de la vie*, but Sainte-Beuve himself furnished the most accurate estimate of the relation between this collection of poems and his own spiritual development. He wrote in the "Table des Lundis": "Les *Consolations* n'ont rien été pour moi qu'une saison morale, six mois célestes et fugitifs dans ma vie."[2] The period of religious intensity characterized by this collection was prolonged with difficulty beyond 1830. Sainte-Beuve's spiritual situation only a few months after publication of the *Consolations* is clarified in André Billy's account of the author's remarks to Juste Olivier on July 21, 1830: "Nous autres, disait Sainte-Beuve, notre foi est toute dans nos vers, en sorte que, quand nous avons fait un volume de vers, toute notre

---

2. Charles-Augustin Sainte-Beuve, *Les Causeries du Lundi*, Vol. XVI: *Table générale et analytique*, ed. Ch. Pierrot (Paris: Garnier Frères, 1880), p. 44.

foi s'y trouve et nous n'en avons plus pour dix ans . . ."[3] Later, in a note added in 1869 to an article on La Rochefoucauld of January 15, 1840, Sainte-Beuve threw some retrospective light upon the religious deviation of 1829 and a return to the positivistic philosophy that he considered more appropriate to maturity:

> Ma première jeunesse, du moment que j'avais commencé à réfléchir, avait été toute philosophique, et d'une philosophie positive en accord avec les études physiologiques et médicales auxquelles je me destinais. Mais une grave affection morale, un grand trouble de sensibilité était intervenu vers 1829, et avait produit une vraie déviation dans l'ordre de mes idées. Mon recueil de poésies, les *Consolations*, et d'autres écrits qui suivirent, notamment *Volupté*, et les premiers volumes de *Port-Royal*, témoignent assez de cette disposition inquiète et émue qui admettait une part notable de mysticisme. L'Étude sur La Rochefoucauld annonce la guérison et marque la fin de cette crise, le retour à des idées plus saines dans lesquelles les années et la réflexion n'ont fait que m'affermir.[4]

If the attraction of Christian religiosity depended upon his feeling of security in Madame Hugo's affections, then its dissolution was probably well under way by the end of 1836, the date of the break in Sainte-Beuve's relations with Adèle. In the meantime, while yet in love, the poet of the *Consolations* had embarked (by the end of 1831) upon his novel *Volupté*.

The emphasis in the *Consolations* upon the earthly felicity of the Christian life does much to explain why the collection was at first unpalatable to Baudelaire. In the early defectiveness of his own Christianity, one of the younger poet's problems was the inability, in his obsession with the idea of ubiquitous sin, to perceive the Christian possibility of a *vie suffisante* in man's world. Massin explains that he tried to satisfy his

3. Billy, *Sainte-Beuve*, I, 109.
4. Charles-Augustin Sainte-Beuve, *Portraits de Femmes* (2nd ed.; Paris: Garnier Frères, 1852), p. 321.

appetite for divine perfection outside the spiritual intimacy of his own soul:

> Tout à l'heure, lorsque *l'enfant* était triomphant encore, lorsque "l'extase de la vie" dominait et soulevait le cœur de Baudelaire, n'était pas encore réduite à cette protestation humble et frénétique à la fois contre "l'horreur," le poète arborait un romantisme autrement lumineux et respirant que ses confrères; il voulait retrouver dans son "intimité," la "couleur" et la "spiritualité" de son "aspiration vers l'infini." Maintenant il s'est identifié pour un long moment au Baudelaire de la légende. Plus d'intimité, puisque son intérieur sert de niche à tous les diables, est visité sans relâche par la succession des *Sept Vieillards!* Plus de recherche précise et volontaire de l'extase lyrique, plus même à l'horizon l'ombre d'un platonicien, mais une fuite éperdue hors de soi, et tant pis pour le quelconque pays où l'on se réfugiera, absent enfin du désert de l'ennui.[5]

On the contrary, Delorme's moral lucidity, having thoroughly explored the *horreur de la vie,* moved forward to the perception of the spiritual alternative implicit in the duality of the soul. The new Delorme of the *Consolations,* while recognizing that the sufferings of the *vie insuffisante* are caused by man's separation from God, was able to attain the treasures of a *vie suffisante* in God's kingdom on earth. These treasures were what they always had been, and must be, for the Christian faith: repentance of sin, prayer to God the Father through the Son, absolution by the passion of the Son, constant recall to vigilance in the soul, and the intervention of divine grace in man's practice of charity. In Christian terms, indulgence of the senses entailed the wanton sacrifice of the soul to eternal damnation. The Christian life secured the triumph in human society of sublime values over profane values. Earthly love nourished in the love of God conquered carnal passion. Humility banished pride. The expectation of immortality in God's

---

5. Massin, *Baudelaire "entre Dieu et Satan,"* pp. 115-116.

eternal kingdom enabled the Christian calmly to accept the tyranny of time. Art created according to the divine intention expunged the disgrace of genius dissipated in the abuses of irresponsible fantasy. Finally the sufferings involved in poetic sterility were transformed into the spiritual ecstasy of poetic creation.

Delorme's *vie suffisante* was never equalled by anything formally expressed in Baudelaire's *Fleurs du Mal* or in his prose poems. The historical facts contain, however, considerably irony. As a Catholic poet and a Christian soul, Sainte-Beuve appears greatly inferior to his disciple. Certainly by 1840 he had espoused that nineteenth-century positivism which embraced a modern heresy particularly inimical to Baudelaire's Catholic theology and to his concept of civilization:

> Toutes les hérésies auxquelles je faisais allusion tout à l'heure ne sont, après tout, que la conséquence de la grande hérésie moderne, de la doctrine *artificielle*, substituée à la doctrine naturelle—je veux dire la suppression de l'idée du *péché originel.*[6]

> Théorie de la vraie civilization. Elle n'est pas dans le gaz, ni dans la vapeur, ni dans les tables tournantes, elle est dans la diminution des traces du péché originel.[7]

Baudelaire's importance as a Catholic poet, on the other hand, was due primarily to his consistent emphasis on original sin and its perpetuation in modern man. The poem "L'imprévu" and the *Journaux intimes* reveal, however, that at least after 1863 he was progressing painfully, but hopefully, toward the conclusion that the effective practice of the Christian faith could offer in this earthly life the *vie suffisante* for which he so ardently yearned.

6. Baudelaire, *Correspondance générale*, I, 370.
7. Baudelaire, "Mon cœur mis à nu," *Œuvres complètes*, II, 752.

4. Bipolarity of the soul in Sainte-Beuve's Volupté

The significance of *Volupté* to Baudelaire, expressed in verses already cited in Chapter 1, must be here re-emphasized as an important element in the formation of his early poetry:

> J'en ai tout absorbé, les miasmes, les parfums,
> Le doux chuchotement des souvenirs défunts,
> Les longs enlacements des phrases symboliques,
>
> . . . .
>
> —Livre voluptueux, si jamais il en fut.—

The terms used in this evaluation suggest that he appreciated the work as a powerful illustration of the phenomenon of moral duality in the human temperament. In the light of Baudelaire's indication, it is precisely as an exposition of moral bipolarity that *Volupté* will be examined in this chapter. However, within a basic framework of moral duality, the psychological subtleties in this novel suggest that the final inertia of the hero's will which precedes his spiritual catharsis results from a moral multivalence which is only ultimately perceived as a duel between the sacred and the profane.

Sainte-Beuve himself, in the preface to the work, described the particular tendency in the human soul that he proposed to analyze:

> Le véritable objet de ce livre est l'analyse d'un penchant, d'une passion, d'un vice même, et de tout le côté de l'âme que ce vice domine, et auquel il donne le ton, du côté languissant, oisif, attachant, secret et privé, mystérieux et furtif, rêveur jusqu'à la subtilité, tendre jusqu'à la mollesse, voluptueux enfin.

Volupté in man, according to Sainte-Beuve, possesses a double nature, in that it is a divine gift corrupted by human perversity —a gift which is potentially both the exaltation and the agony of modern youth:

> Don corrompu du Créateur, vestige, emblème et gage d'un autre amour, trésor pernicieux et cher qu'il nous faut porter dans une sainte ignorance, ensevelir à jamais, s'il se peut, sous nos manteaux obscurs, et qu'on doit, si l'on en fait usage, ménager chastement comme le sel le plus blanc de l'autel, la volupté a été pour vous de bonne heure un vœu brillant, une fleur humide, une grappe savoureuse où montaient vos désirs, l'aliment unique en idée, la couronne de votre jeunesse. (p. 4)

That which originally seduces emotionally awakened adolescence is pursued, because of its evasiveness, to the point where the pursuit becomes a habit. Yet the fatiguing monotony of this habit does not reduce its domination. The passage through the stage of seduction, so the hero Amaury advises his readers, is common to any rising generation. Rather than the seduction, it is the issue therefrom which is vitally important to the moral individual: "C'est à l'issue qu'il convient de s'attacher; c'est dans le mode d'impression intime qu'on reçoit de ces traverses, et dans la moralité pratique qu'on en tire, que consiste notre signe original et distinctif, notre mérite propre, notre vertu avec l'aide de Dieu" (p. 6).

In the initial state of moral hysteria, voluptuous youth desires all that flatters the senses. Profane desire is confused with sacred love. Youth must taste the sensual pleasures. But the wisdom of experience ever reminds mature man that in resulting grief or disgust the experiments of the young always bear witness to the essential divorce of sublime love from sensual profaneness. Beauty itself is scourged and vilified by the passions.

In his verses to Sainte-Beuve of 1844, Baudelaire referred to a special art of creating *volupté* even out of suffering:

> Et, devant le miroir, j'ai perfectionné
> L'art cruel qu'un démon, en naissant, m'a donné,
> —De la douleur pour faire une volupté vraie,—
> D'ensanglanter un mal et de gratter sa plaie.

When Amaury first realizes that he is no longer emotionally sterile, he is similarly moved to indulge his tender feelings by renewing the exquisite pains of a jealous and illicit love. For without such a renewal, persistent pains become a mere habit. Indeed, he might even fail to recognize a love which seldom had the opportunity to try itself. The subtle monotony of endless unrequited feelings finally persuades Amaury that he is, in fact, only skirting rather than fulfilling his own existence. He is to discover later that these wounds are but silently undermining the strength of his will.

After finally succumbing to the lure of the prostitute, Sainte-Beuve's hero becomes subtly aware of the dual polarity in moral man. Many years later a wiser Amaury confesses to his pupil that, once having been promiscuous, he began to recognize that in life there are two different stages of youth, one following the other:

la première, exubérante, ascendante, se suffisant toujours, ne croyant pas à la fatigue, n'en faisant nul compte, embrassant à la fois les choses contraires, et lançant de front tous ses coursiers. Il y en a une seconde, déjà fatiguée et avertie, qui conserve presque les mêmes dehors, mais à qui une voix crie souvent holà! en dedans; qui ne cède guère qu'à regret, se repent vite d'avoir cédé, et ne mène plus d'un train égal l'esprit et le corps tout ensemble. (p. 125)

Amaury notes a far too abrupt swing of the moral pendulum between "une vie inférieure, submergée, engloutie" and "une vie plus active de tête et de cœur." There is a rapid alternation from "la convulsion grossière" to an "aspiration platonique." This moral shifting eventually proves fatal to man's spiritual faith and to sublime love. Man's will to act no longer has any support and his moral personality is reduced to a mere "composé délié, de courants et de fluides, un amas mobile et tournoyant, une scène commode à mille jeux."

The ruin of the inner man is effected by processes of erosion and corrosion with which Amaury becomes only too familiar in the course of his lascivious expeditions. The first lesson he learns—one of several producing an aggregate of fruitless knowledge—concerns the fatal beauty that seduces man's senses:

c'est une beauté réelle, mais accablante et toute de chair, qui semble remonter en droite ligne aux filles des premières races déchues, qui ne se juge point en face et en conversant de vive voix, ainsi qu'il convient à l'homme, mais de loin plutôt, sur le hasard de la nuque et des reins, comme ferait le coup d'œil du chasseur pour les bêtes sauvages: oh! j'ai compris cette beauté-là. (p. 127)

A second lesson establishes that this type of beauty, while creating the maximum disorders in the senses, provokes the weakest possible reaction in the soul. Thence it follows, in a further lesson, that the impermanent nature of feminine beauty led him from one woman to another, spurred on by disgust with the preceding one. Thus, "la volupté cruelle et qui boit le sang" enters man through his eyes, which are the windows of his soul. By the slow corruption of the spirit, man's other faculties are swept into an unholy fusion with sensual gratification. The very substance of the soul is wasted by an insidious softening, though no overt act of vice be committed. Inveighing against the materialistic acceptance of sensual passion as a necessary hygiene quite independent of the rest of man's moral behavior, Sainte-Beuve points austerely to the enormity of the spiritual disaster involved in the cult of sensuality. He indicates that for man's true life in the soul, every rebound in the direction of sensual vice is a profound moral tragedy. This tragedy lies in the dissipation of man's highest potential in intellectual genius, in fruitful intentions, in human compassion, and in the works of charity.

Amaury realizes that he fell into the error of attaching all happiness to a system of lax living, resorting thus to a cure which was itself a sickness fatal to the soul. In this spiritual laxity where God was thrust into the background, sensual diversion easily replaced moral solicitude. The troublesome prospect of the immediate future, indeed of all eternity, disappeared in the titillating moment. But such a concession to the profane yielded to a bitter vexation in the realization that all the chaos of evil had been experienced without tasting of its coarse and superficial attractions. With retrospective wisdom, Amaury is anxious to warn his young friend of the terrible bondage of carnal pleasure. Such diversion, in its failure to fulfil the high promise of early passion, leads inevitably to disenchantment: " 'Vous n'ignorez pas quel dégoût suit la volupté, quelle nonchalance elle inspire, quel oubli profond des devoirs, quels frivoles soins, quelles craintes, quelles distractions insensées!' " (p. 163).

In his portrayal of Amaury, Sainte-Beuve offers a most penetrating analysis of the insidious invasion of vice into man's moral stronghold. Carnal sin destroys the humility and the lucidity of his hero, undermining the very foundations of his moral structure:

> C'est que, malgré toutes les velléités de conscience, tous les élans et les soupirs d'en haut, rien de suivi, de désintéressé et de pur n'était praticable avec cette secousse de l'abîme, avec cet écroulement fréquent et caché. Qu'importe de veiller et d'observer au front des tours, et d'interroger les étoiles, si le traître et le lâche livrent à chaque instant la porte souter-raine par où pénètrent les eaux? (pp. 204-205)

In Amaury's relationship with Madame de Couaën, the insin-uating voice of profane *volupté* urges escape from the bonds of a spirituality which has become too suffocating. The young *voluptueux* begins to covet "cette émancipation moitié or-gueilleuse et moitié sensuelle." Paralyzed in a sudden aridity of sentiment, he realizes that his idol cannot satisfy that inde-finable desire for something more, "non pas autre chose d'elle, mais autre chose qu'elle." At this point he experiences the ennui shared by all lovers, which results from the weakness of man's nature. His love for Madame de Couaën is demonstrably selfish, inasmuch as he begrudges what seems to him her timidity and her preoccupation with her own family: "Et je lui en voulais d'une si admirable sensibilité de mère, non seule-ment comme d'un tort fait à ce que je prétendais être pour elle, mais comme d'une fatigue qui brûlait sa joue de veilles et qui altérait sa beauté!" (p. 221). The object of his passion never seems even conscious of his spiteful reaction or of the con-trivings of his self-esteem.

In examining the subtle process of his own moral collapse, Amaury is careful to distinguish between an earlier stage of in-terior sin and a subsequent overt consummation of desire. As for merely savoring the maturing thought of evil, he observes:

> L'émotion prolongée, que je me donnais au sein du péril, était donc relevée d'une sorte de sécurité précaire et d'un

faux reste d'innocence. C'était toujours la même façon ruineuse de pousser à bout au dedans, de mûrir, de *pourrir* presque en moi la pensée du mal avant l'acte, d'amonceler mille ferments mortels avant de rien produire. (p. 123)

Amaury knows that the exterior act of transgression could be a compensation for those minor wrongs and frustrations in life whereby man is lowered to intoxication and to animal satisfaction. But there is also that occasion when the sheer insanity of profane passion and the consciousness of certain evil drives him to sin. Then the *voluptueux* is seized by something more sinister than sensual pleasure. He becomes governed by a satanic pride in his own fall, a competitive urge in the perpetration of evil and a sense of revolt against the law of God.

What account can Amaury give to the severe moral rectitude of Amélie de Liniers when she asks the results of his two-year search for some solution to his moral disequilibrium? In place of a recaptured virility of the spirit, he can unfold only the wretched history of a desperate spiritual disintegration, in which the happiness of others as well as his own has been wantonly sacrificed. He is tortured by the paralyzing perplexity of his own well-intentioned youth caught in the snare of illicit desire, no longer able to choose between virtue and vice. Such an agony, in which the soul is both trophy and battlefield, seems to him characteristic of his generation:

Agonie, rapetissement, et plaintes des âmes tendres déchues! Oh! j'ai bien connu cette situation fausse et son absurde profondeur, ces dégoûts de tout qu'elle engendre, cet embrouillement inextricable qui meurtrit bientôt sur tous les points un cerveau jusque-là sain, net et vigoureux, cet échec perpétuel au principe et au ressort de toute action, cette lente et muette défaite au sein des années vaillantes! C'est comme un combat qui se livre incessamment en nous sans pouvoir se trancher d'un côté ni de l'autre, et l'âme en prostration, qui est le prix du combat, sert aussi de champ de

> bataille et subit tous les refoulements contraires, et ne sait,
> à la fin de chaque journée, à qui elle appartient! (p. 248)

The paralysis of the will is aggravated, moreover, by the pernicious practice of idle dreaming, which Amaury has substituted for the humble but forceful discipline of Christian prayer.

In the case of Sainte-Beuve's hero, spiritual inertia results from a psychological multivalence which tends to resolve itself into a dual polarity of the psyche. From generalizations applicable to a whole young generation, this multivalence is translated into a system depending on the counter-attractions of specific personalities in Amaury's life. At the most potentially fruitful period of his manhood, he finds himself drawn alternately to three women, as if to three towers in the nether region of Limbo. But this perplexity is always without issue, becoming the punishment of an unredeemed abuse of youth's highest promise. Thus, Madame R——, representing the profane pole of Amaury's spiritual dualism, introduces destructive discord into the harmonious spirituality of the hero's relationships with Amélie de Liniers and Madame de Couaën:

> Pour moi, en qui toutes vibrations aboutissaient, il m'était clair que les deux premières âmes de sœurs s'éloignèrent avec un frémissement de colombes blessées, sitôt que la troisième survint; que cette troisième se sentit à la gêne aussi et tremblante, quoique légèrement aggressive; il me parut que la pieuse union du concert ébauché fit place à une discordance, à un tiraillement pénible, et que nous nous mîmes, tous les quatre, à palpiter et à saigner. (p. 267)

Yet, in studying closely the character of this lady from the beginning of her relationship with Amaury, one cannot fail to appreciate the complexity of her position at the pole of profane love. Madame R—— is not a participant in the ultimate vice of carnal indulgence, but rather personifies an illusion of profane passion necessary to the affective constitution of the hero.

[66]

Her function is fulfilled between his sublime love for Madame de Couaën and the sheer bestiality of his crudest Parisian encounters. She inspires, however, a particularly perfidious form of infidelity, in that it is intellectual rather than sensual.

The ascendancy of Madame R—— over the hero results from a highly subjective interplay of emotions originating in the excessive strain of his equivocal situation between spiritual love and sensual pleasure:

> une voix moqueuse me rappelait tout bas, d'un ton de mondaine sagesse, que j'étais las à l'excès de l'amitié sans la possession et de la possession sans amour. J'avais beau éviter de peser sur l'idée perfide, il m'arrivait, chaque fois que la visite avait lieu, de regarder plus volontiers du côté de cette faible étoile qui brillait dans les yeux de Mme R——. (p. 170)

At the outset, Amaury does little more than enjoy the flattering sensation of pleasing two women without necessarily exhausting his capacity for feeling. Subsequently, owing to his involvement in the conspiracy of General Georges, his life assumes a precariousness which seems to justify a desire to be openly loved before death. For such a superficial satisfaction, he has little hesitation in choosing Madame R—— over Madame de Couaën. However, the effective execution of this choice is thereafter nullified by the failure of the Georges conspiracy and the unexpected creation of a new understanding with Madame de Couaën prior to her departure from Paris. The contemplated declaration of passion to Madame R—— finally destroyed, her role in Amaury's life is destined to develop in a very different climate from that envisaged earlier.

During a period of continence following the departure of the Couaën family, Amaury visits Madame R—— rarely. Only as a result of his relapse into carnal promiscuity does her reparative function come into operation. An hour or so of affable but artificial gallantry suffices to cover a sensual transgression by a less crude but more treasonable cerebral perfidy. This more subtle moral poison seems even to ennoble the disorder of the soul. By the collusion of mental and sensual treachery, promiscuous indulgence, whereas initially it had caused a withdrawal to a more refined "duplicité riante et perfide," becomes again in its turn the natural consequence of that same particularized betrayal. All this sophistry, moreover, continues in fact to be dominated by the Beatrice-like influence of Madame de Couaën.

The sovereignty of Madame R—— is yet to know certain triumphs before its final eclipse. A brief visit to his Beatrice in her new domicile convinces Amaury that "les pures amitiés durables avec les jeunes femmes" are impossible, except under conditions intolerable to the men who adore them. In his frustration, the picture of Madame R—— assumes a new vitality for him. She permits him to rejoin the broken ties of the earlier relationship; but by refusing to share the delirium of his passion, she ensures the bitter lesson of its failure. This experience teaches him that even the most lighthearted amatory adventure leaves a permanent scar on the heart:

> Quoi qu'on en juge d'abord, toutes ces liaisons à l'accès riant, toutes ces épreuves de tendresse nous sont rudement comptées; elles ne se succèdent pas en nous impunies; si l'engagement est léger, le changement est accablant et amer; quand l'essai rompt, la marque demeure et fait cicatrice avec souffrance ou endurcissement. (pp. 228-229)

The restraint of Madame R——, owing much to her awareness of Madame de Couaën's continuing rivalry, is partially relaxed by Amaury's reiterated renunciation of his Beatrice. Her enjoyment of her apparent triumph, nevertheless, is disciplined by a vigilant lucidity. Whereas other women would be silent or incoherent before the passionate avowals of their lovers, she has the composure to observe herself, even at the very center of her emotional agitation. Her languor is not, Amaury subsequently notes, the vague and transcendental reverie of

Madame de Couaën. On the contrary, it is motivated by "une multitude de petites tristesses positives, de petits désirs souffrants et de piqûres mal fermées sur mille points." Such preoccupations, rather than a capacity for love, explain the complicated structure of her personality. Gradually, she exposes that shallowness and frailty of heart which are finally to convince her lover that it is Madame de Couaën whom he really loves and who is most capable of loving him. He discovers that Madame R—— and he have fallen among those souls who are impoverished and eroded by a longing for appearance rather than for essence. A complete breakdown of confidence between the two is not slow to follow Amaury's discovery, without, however, bringing to an abrupt conclusion their futile liaison. His aim, henceforth, is gradually to slacken the bonds between them, but without any shock to bruise either heart. The possibility of terminating their relationship smoothly proves to be an illusion. He is wounded in his self-esteem by her failure to "assembler en une liaison choisie assez d'âme et de sens, assez de vice et de délicatesse." In his possession, she is just a confused creature with a capacity inadequate either for loving or for being loved. Her inadequacy provokes him to an irritation exacerbated by the remorse which, in a tender soul, normally follows a relapse into carnal pleasure. His brutal egoism finally explodes in a cruel reproach. By the scene of physical violence that follows, Madame R—— is at last convinced of the possibility of a definite rupture in their association. Her lover, in his turn, recognizes irrevocably the true nature of profane passion:

L'astuce impure a ses grossièretés par où finalement elle se trahit. La boue des cœurs humains remonte et trouble tout dans ces luttes dernières, dans ces secousses où de factices passions se dépouillent et s'avouent. L'égoïsme de la nature sensuelle se produit hideusement, soit qu'il bouillonne en écume de colère, soit qu'il dégoutte en une lie lente et glacée. On arrive, au tournant des pentes riantes, à des fonds de marais ou à des sables. (p. 282)

The aftermath of the rupture is Amaury's return, more vulnerable than ever, to the promiscuous indulgence of carnal desire. From these exploits he comes to the sobering consciousness of the poverty of real love in the *voluptueux*. There he found only superficial tears, only a semblance of compassion. The energy which should have been spent in catholic charity toward his fellow man has been wasted in greedy self-indulgence. The wanton dissipation of his vitality and the countless relapses into vice leave him with a deep sense of exhaustion and inertia. This moment, when his entire being is receptive to an interior voice of conscience or the declaration of a universal lament, mark the passing of his first youth. He is appalled by the enormity of his personal void, and yet momentarily filled more with shame at his personal degradation than with remorse toward the God whose grace could guide him through the chaos of his spirit. Over this atmosphere of contrition Madame de Couaën resumes her henceforth indomitable yet remote command.

After the final break with Madame R——, Amaury undertakes to prune one by one the impediments to a more sublime course for his life. Casting aside the fleeting ties of worldly pleasure, which he had accepted only for her sake, he feels the infinite expansiveness of freedom. Yet he records that it was not an unqualified deliverance. Even as he pursues his painful way to a purer existence, his will stumbles under the temptations of the *démon avant-coureur* and the *démon de midi*. There are delays in his return to God.

Among the last impediments in the movement toward spiritual rehabilitation is a final skirmish with that ancient enemy, *la gloire*. Amaury had, in fact, been subject to its seductive power from the beginning of his formation as a *voluptueux*. The introspection of his boyhood emanated in part from a sense of isolation from the drama of the times, from the festival of France's resurgence under Bonaparte. His resistance to the political and religious ideas of contemporary society caused the early emergence of a strong individualism. But for the energies of this individual genius, there was no outlet in a dead royalist cause. There was only a semblance of action in a "torrent de vœux et de regrets aux heures les plus oisives." Although the sharp points of ambition never really ceased to irritate the smooth surface of a languorous *volupté*, the spiritual side of Amaury's nature becomes again conscious, on the eve of the Georges conspiracy, that purely human honor has scant morality. He is forced to admit, albeit without repentance, the preponderance of egotism in his project of glory. Later, his abortive ride to Strasbourg to join Napoleon's victorious armies clearly assumes the form of a delirious spiritual relapse. The complex of guilt in the pursuit of glory represents, long before the hero's final catharsis, an incipient tendency away from worldly values to those of the sublime *extase*.

Though the first ardor of his sensual appetites has been extinguished, the depths of the abyss fail to insulate Amaury from the insistent murmur of man's need for the spiritual reality of love. In what he describes as second youth, a voice proclaims man's capacity for the Infinite and his power to love. The nature of the sole love worthy of his potential reveals itself to the former sinner in his spiritual regeneration. He is able to identify it in terms of a virility peculiar to Christian charity and foreign to the sensual delights of the profane vanities. He finds it ever circumspect, humble, and upright; neither soft, nor lighthearted, nor given to frivolities; sober, chaste, stable, filled with quietness, and guarded by sentries at the gates of the senses. In contrast to carnal passion, this love is innocent of selfish interests. At the sublime pole of his spiritual duality, but still participating in his terrestrial existence, this spirit of charity serves as a herald of divine love. It knows neither exhaustion nor respite in its work of distributing among human souls the beneficent nourishment of God's ultimate goodness. At the great crises of man's life, where in suffering or death the ultimate truth is perceived in terms of God's love, the intrusion of man's baser nature would seem like the exhalation of the sewers in a big city. Clearly the Almighty, at His chosen times, reimmerses mortal man in the sobering waters of His ultimate reality, that man might purge himself of the idolatrous joys of the flesh. Experience teaches that man's freedom is significant only as a grasp of that ultimate reality, for his freedom depends upon his power to place or not to place himself under the control of material objectivity.

Spiritual reintegration also reveals to Sainte-Beuve's erstwhile degenerate hero that he has never before understood Saint-Martin's dictum that "l'homme naît et vit dans les pensées." At the sublime pole of man's existence, Amaury now discovers a whole system of symbols by which the meaning of the Divine Creation may be interpreted to mortal man within it:

> Toutes les choses visibles du monde et de la nature, toutes les œuvres et tous les êtres, outre leur signification matérielle, de première vue, d'ordre élémentaire et d'utilité, me parurent acquérir la signification morale d'une pensée, —de quelque pensée d'harmonie, de beauté, de tristesse, d'attendrissement, d'austérité ou d'admiration. Et il était au pouvoir de mon sens moral intérieur, en s'y dirigeant, d'interpréter ou du moins de soupçonner ces signes divers, de cueillir ou du moins d'odorer les fruits du verger mystérieux, de dégager quelques syllabes de cette grande parole qui, fixée ici, errante là, frémissait partout dans la nature. (p. 160)

But the majority of ordinary men, even though talented and enjoying worldly renown, live beneath that mask of false reality which is afforded by the immediate sense impression. For them "ne sentir nullement les ondulations de cette vraie atmosphère qui nous baignent" or "y rester glacé, s'en préserver comme d'un mauvais air, et fermer les canaux supérieurs de l'esprit à ces influences aimables qui le veulent nourrir" are moral possibilities.

Even in the course of his spiritual progress, the possibility of relapse is too great for Amaury not to realize that chastity is a co-operative achievement of mortal will and divine grace. In the most saintly among men, spiritual initiative is steadily supported by the lead strings of the Holy Spirit. For the less saintly, in whom the will to piety proves more feeble, God's grace persists as a spiritual conscience, suspending or neutralizing the urge to sin. A particularly illuminating example of the coincidence of divine grace with human will marks the beginning of Amaury's spiritual reformation. The confrontation of the three most important women in the drama of his life suggests the inevitability of Madame R——'s eclipse to the advantage of Madame de Couaën. Though not immediately intelligible to him, God's design is clearly involved in this occurrence, suspended over his head, awaiting his eventual comprehension. For this sinner striving toward moral resurrection, Madame de Couaën is a special agent to implement the fusion of mortal desire and grace in a sublime ecstasy.

Among the great influences in Amaury's catharsis is his faith in the miraculous works of the Abbé Carron. This ecclesiastic, he concludes, is surely a special medium for the intervention of the Holy Spirit in the affairs of men—a chosen being in whose life God's mysterious designs are manifested to man in superhuman acts. From the inspiration of the Abbé Carron's exemplary spirituality, it is not a long step, by way of Christian reading, to the austere Jansenist virtue of Port-Royal. The instinct of the acolyte inherent in Amaury's spiritual diffidence moves him to choose as master Monsieur Hamon, a member of the Port-Royal community deeply revered by Racine. To him, to the Abbé Carron and to Saint-Martin, the regenerate *voluptueux* owes a spiritual gift which proves to be the edification of his dissipated life:

> Ce don consiste à retrouver Dieu et son intention vivante partout, jusque dans les moindres détails et les plus petits mouvements, à ne perdre jamais du doigt un certain ressort qui conduit. Tout prend alors un sens, un enchaînement particulier, une vibration infiniment subtile qui avertit, un commencement de nouvelle lumière. La trame invisible, qui est la base spirituelle de la Création et des causes secondes, qui se continue à travers tous les événements et les fait jouer en elle comme un simple épanouissement de sa surface, ou si l'on veut, comme des franges pendantes, cette trame profonde devient sensible en plusieurs endroits, et toujours certaine là même où elle se dérobe. . . . Dans cette disposition intérieure de spiritualité, la vigilance est perpétuelle; pas un point ne reste indifférent autour de nous pour le but divin; tout grain de sable reluit. (pp. 320-321)

Amaury's new Christian perspective seems to close the circle of his spiritual wandering. He had been trained since infancy to accept certain religious dogma. This intellectual assent had been corrupted first by the philosophical curiosity of youth; but in the final analysis, his revolt against Christian tradition is in his departure from a pure moral life. In the moment of reconversion, his thoughts turn to those whose tender hearts were wounded by his decadent behavior, and especially to Madame de Couaën. Recomposing in his soul the sublime passion, he feels the need for some particular expiation of his sin—a penance which, in relation to her, will be both "une barrière et un canal sacrés." Anxious to bring his ideal love into harmony with his religion, he is in haste to "mettre l'idée de Mme de Couaën en toute sûreté et pureté sur l'autel." His final decision to enter the seminary is the implementation of this desire, whose object he now sees as the holy sacraments and orders of the Church.

Just as Madame R—— represents a particular intrusion of

profane love, so Madame de Couaën personifies the sublime pole in Amaury's moral duality. The conditions of their relationship are dictated by the exacting spirituality of her temperament, inasmuch as all of his moral tendencies are illumined by the degree of their harmony or disharmony with the affective ideals that she established.

The earliest contacts between Amaury and the woman who was to become his Beatrice are characterized by a refined respect and a reluctance on his part to examine the nature of his own sentiments toward her. In fact, the first contours of her chaste image are fixed, not in his private thoughts, but in his conversations with others concerning her. Only gradually and imperceptibly does her spiritual beauty captivate the curiosity of his soul. It is only when this undercurrent of interest becomes intensified into a specific passion that the first note of discord is sounded in the relationship. Thereafter, the actions and attitudes of Madame de Couaën for a long time exert an aggravating resistance to the emotional initiative of her lover. The mysterious spiritual strength which he feels to emanate from his love for her does not dispel his impatience with an intolerable atmosphere of dissimulation. He experiences a frequent urge proudly to rattle the chain of his enslavement, neither hiding nor breaking the bond of love. She, for her part, imposes upon him a loyalty of severe self-abnegation:

> "Oh! promettez que vous ne partirez jamais, me disait-elle; M. de Couaën vous aime tant! vous nous êtes nécessaire. Ma mère n'est plus, j'ai besoin de vous pour vous parler d'elle et de ces choses que vous seul savez écouter .... Dites, vous resterez avec nous toujours, vous ne vous marierez jamais!" (p. 72)

During the crisis following her husband's arrest, Madame de Couaën appears to accept her admirer's services with passive docility. Amaury becomes increasingly bewildered by the enigma of sensitivity and depth which he finds in the apathy

of his Beatrice. He is in the habit of picturing her as an un-
fathomable lake, alternately calm and agitated by the ripples
of a secret anguish. He feels, with a mixture of sickening discouragement and superstitious abandon, that this lake seldom
reflects him. He grants that the small sacrifice of his attentions
to her is amply repaid by rapid and lucid moments of pure
felicity which fill his journeys homeward from her presence.
Such moments do not, however, create a reliable spiritual
state. Under the pressure of practical action, his very devotion
comes to lack the gracious smile and the tenderness of lan-
guage. It becomes a gloomy, hurried and exhausted devotion,
into which the slave's persistent urge to freedom intrudes
itself. The desire for freedom is inspired by new enthusiasms:
by the atmosphere of the Parisian scene with its constant
appeals to ambition and to the senses; by Madame de Couaën's
apparent indifference and her firm absorption in more legiti-
mate thoughts. While they await her husband's release from
prison, there are some happy days when her lover seems to
be included in her plans, but the stronger impression is that
of a veil suspended between them. Her normal indifference
is occasionally relieved by an anxious concern for Amaury's
changing conduct and ideas. The basis of her anxiety is a
certain mobility in thought and in taste, which the profane
sophistication of Paris seems to be developing in him. His
newly acquired enthusiasms suggest to her the possibility of
some future change in their association.

In the face of Madame de Couaën's persistent inability to
comprehend the reasons for his reluctance to participate in her
future life as an exile at Blois, Amaury is driven to counter
her accusation of lukewarm affection by an unprecedented
confession of his hopeless passion:

> "Vous ne voyez dans mon incertitude de vous rejoindre
> qu'une preuve qu'on vous aime moins; n'y pourriez-vous lire
> plus justement une crainte qu'on a de vous aimer trop? Sup-

posez par grâce, un moment, que quelqu'un en soit venu à craindre de trop aimer un Etre de pureté et de devoir, hors de toute portée, et en qui cette pensée même qu'on puisse l'aimer ainsi n'entre pas, et dites, après, si ces contradictions de conduite et de volonté, qui vous blessent, ne deviennent pas explicables." (p. 190)

When he warns his beloved that the pure ardor of selfless adoration would be followed by a series of importunate advances, she finds it less disturbing to regard this warning as a mere intellectual display. It is easy for her to convince him that his passion is not so serious a transgression that it could not be mitigated by her vigilant help. To appease the profane desires that he claims are consuming him, she proffers the precious conceit of imagining the satisfaction of those appetites, thus strangling desire in its infancy. It is then Amaury's turn to prolong the mutual deception of two hearts by a subtlety of his own. If he can be convinced that the physical consummation of his love for her is hopeless, his passion will dissolve in its very discouragement. So effective is the total illusion that, by the time of the Couaëns' departure for Blois, he is completely captivated by the mollifying ingenuousness of his countess. He returns to the serious contemplation of a life of sacrifice, devoted to the exiles in their midst.

The spirit of dedication, and the promise of future happiness that it seems to hold, are belied by the lover's subsequent conduct. The first year of exile is marked by extreme vacillation in the soul of Amaury. Rebellion against the sterility of a passion which Madame de Couaën is unwilling to return or even recognize drives him into the final treacherous liaison with Madame R——. Rebellion in turn against the enslavement of this relationship inspires a renewed desire on his part to return to the Beatrice at Blois. This return would have proved irresistible, were it not for the tragedy which brings Madame de Couaën temporarily back to Paris.

The death of her son can only be understood by the countess as divine punishment for the illegitimacy of even a spiritual alliance with Amaury. This interpretation is the culmination of a pre-existing disquiet on this subject which has disturbed her ever since the exile to Blois. Yet she cannot resist the compulsion to seek spiritual solace from her lover in her bereavement. Surveying with him the fate which has befallen their promises and plans for happiness of nearly a year ago, she seems to seek some austere lesson for them both in the contrast between the impressions of former times and those of the present moment. This severe examination produces a very clear image of the deception to which a soul destined for the sublime love of the spirit is exposed in the world of man:

> Elle disait qu'il y a un jour dans la vie de l'âme où l'on a trente ans; que les choses apparaissent alors ce qu'elles sont; que cette illusion d'amour qui, sous la forme d'un bel oiseau bleu, a voltigé devant nous, sauté et reculé sans cesse pour nous inviter à avancer, nous voyant, au milieu, bien engagés dans la forêt et les ronces, s'envole tout de bon; qu'on ne le distingue plus que de loin par moments au ciel, fixé en étoile qui nous dit de venir; que, vivrait-on alors trente ans encore et trente autres sur cette terre, ce serait toujours de même, et que le mieux serait donc de mourir, s'il plaisait à Dieu, avant d'avoir épuisé cette uniformité; qu'on deviendrait même ainsi plus utile à ceux d'en bas en priant pour eux.
> (p. 257)

The essence of her present spiritual anguish is that the "oiseau d'espérance" has returned to her at age thirty in the person of Amaury. For a brief period, reality and illusion pursue each other from hour to hour in her soul, only to leave her in the final melancholy of disillusion. The dream world of her ideal life, impervious to the corruption of the material world, now suddenly but irrevocably has collapsed.

The spiritual intimacy re-established between Amaury and

his Beatrice is marred, for the rest of her stay in Paris, by her discovery of the real depth that has existed in her lover's alliance with Madame R——. Some obstacle tacitly prevents the pure harmony of their exchanges from that moment. He explains this profane liaison as the result of his desperate need to dull in oblivion the pains of frustration in his more sublime love. She recognizes gratefully his well-intentioned attempt to repair their deteriorating association, but she experiences also a sense of guilt in her backward glance at their former ties. This particular period in their relationship ends, in the event, on a sublime note. A few days after her return to Blois, Madame de Couaën sends her lover the keepsake she has promised. Amaury accepts it as the highest expression of their timeless spiritual union: "Pas de lettre d'ailleurs; des reliques de sa mère et de son enfant, de l'innocent et de la sainte ravis, ce qu'elle avait de plus éternel et de plus pleuré, n'était-ce pas d'elle à moi en ce moment tout un langage sans parole, inépuisable et permis, et le seul fidèle?" (p. 272).

As a spiritual influence upon Amaury at the pole of the *extase*, Madame de Couaën remains apart from the grievous sequence of events attending his final break with Madame R——. Her intercessory power begins to operate again only in the moral abyss where he finds himself after that rupture. He records that her counsel to him at this point, through the medium of Madame de Cursy, is one of two clear signs which point toward a regenerate life of piety, withdrawn from the temptations of the world:

Après ce mot de souvenir à mon intention, elle ajoutait: 'Dites-lui, ma bonne tante, vous qui savez si bien la douceur de l'acceptation volontaire, dites-lui ce que le cœur pieux gagne en bonheur à une vie simplifiée.' Oui, je voulais simplifier ma vie, en accepter les ruines récentes, en rétablir les fondements en un lieu haut et sacré, d'où l'étoile du matin s'apercevrait à chaque réveil .... Cet élan de douloureux conseils s'ajoutant à la sobre et sainte parole de Mme de Couaën, cette rencontre précise de deux avis venus de si loin à la fois, me parut un signe non équivoque. (pp. 290-291)

Thereafter, his twofold desire is to secure his ideal love for the countess in the purity of the Christian religion and to implement her counsel by choosing the ministry of the Church.

The final sanctification of his relationship with her is revealed to Amaury in the providential circumstances of his role at her deathbed. Their simultaneous presence on the family estate in Brittany is an event designed by divine grace for a special purpose of absolute good. The nature of his ministry at this critical moment is paradoxical. From his own inadequate spiritual resources he has to find the strength necessary to raise the soul of his beloved in sacrifice to God at the moment of death. But from the instant of her soul's ascent, the intercessory function returns to his Beatrice:

> Moi qui vous ai aidée, soulevée avec effort et autorité jusque là-haut, du moment que vous y êtes, je retombe, je m'incline; c'est à moi plutôt de vous prier. Secourez-nous, belle Ame, devant Dieu; demandez-lui pour nous la force que nous vous avons communiquée peut-être, mais, hélas! sans l'avoir assez en nous-même; et puisqu'il faut à l'infirmité mortelle, pour marcher constamment vers les sentiers sûrs, un signal, un appel, un souvenir, Ame chaste et chère, intercédez près du Maître pour que vous nous soyez ce souvenir d'au-delà, cette croix apparente aux angles des chemins, pour que vous soyez de préférence l'esprit d'avertissement et l'ange qu'il nous envoie! (p. 367)

At the end of Sainte-Beuve's novel, the spiritual will of his hero is firmly established in the field of the sublime pole. In a life of Christian piety, Amaury attains to the true *extase de la vie*. Yet the multivalence in his psyche imposes a highly devious route on his progress toward that final destination.

The deviations of this complicated itinerary are best explained by the imbalance within his soul of three categories of love: *agape, eros,* and V*enus.* Agape is here intended to define divine love—the source of absolute good—which flows from God to man and, in return, from man both back to God and outward to other men. Eros refers to the lover's desire for, and pre-occupation with, the beloved, implying the negation of him-self and, if necessary, of his carnal desires. Venus is intended to suggest carnal desire alone—a largely animal phenomenon which can be, but not always is, associated with the more cerebral passion of eros.

The relationship between the hero and Madame de Couaën was initially based, for his part, on eros in unduly heavy pro-portion. The lover allowed too much play to his imagination and to his mental preoccupation with the beloved. On the contrary, her response to his erotic exaltation could only be— by reason of her temperament and her obligations to husband and children—an emphasis on agape. Her formidable spirit-uality tended to frustrate her lover's normal yearning for the balanced fusion of soul, mind, and body, which is suggested by the Christian ideal in love between man and woman. The despair resulting from this frustration drove Amaury to seek oblivion in promiscuous encounters on the streets of Paris— a type of sensual gluttony which could not even be dignified by the name of Venus. Horrified by the sordid world of the prostitute, he sought to retrieve, in a liaison with Madame R——, at least the illusion of an eros adequately balanced by Venus. The promiscuous was to be elevated to the particular. Since, however, this amatory charade was seriously lacking in agape, even the illusion of eros was brutally destroyed in conflicts between the selfish interests of the two lovers. The unarticulated coexistence of mutually antagonistic passions in the hero's psyche produced a total inertia in his will to live. In Sainte-Beuve's particular interpretation of the Romantic agony, the *horreur de la vie* results from Amaury's inability to properly infuse agape into his experiences of eros. The illicit nature of his love for Madame de Couaën was itself a serious obstacle to the adequate functioning of agape. The insistent voice of the beloved's spirituality, reproving the hero's most serious moral lapses, promised nothing for the natural love in eros. When the power of agape was eventually reasserted—through the examples of Jansenist piety in Port-Royal and by the injunctions of the countess herself—the translation to the sublime pole of the *extase* was inspired by a spirituality divorced from the world.

As early as 1838 Baudelaire claimed to have a clear understanding of the spiritual multivalence involved in his predecessor's novel. The younger poet's "parfums," found in the verses cited at the beginning of the present chapter, implied both the supernatural ecstasy of the soul inspired by agape and the false ecstasy of the more natural preoccupations of eros and Venus. The "miasmes" implied all the *horreur de la vie* which results from the disequilibrium of agape, eros, and Venus in man's affective experience. The *Fleurs du Mal* indicate the completeness of Baudelaire's education in the torments of mortal sin. His personal sufferings more than confirmed the truth of the original lessons to be learned from Sainte-Beuve's *Volupté*. Subsequent chapters in this study will demonstrate that Amaury's transition from moral despair to the true ecstasy of Christian spirituality was only partially reproduced in the younger poet's case. In conscious need of agape, Baudelaire was never able to achieve it in sufficient measure to repair his broken life. An important factor in this failure was his defective understanding of divine grace and its function in relation to the sinner. The Christian issue from the abyss of spiritual inertia, which is presented in Sainte-Beuve's poems and novel, is not formally proposed in the poetic creation of Baudelaire, nor is it more than vaguely reflected in his personal life. What is clear in the 1861 edition of the *Fleurs du Mal* is the theological gravity of the poet's situation upon the termination of the cycle of spleen. Under the intolerable oppression of the horror that pervades a *vie insuffisante*, the urgent need of the sublime alternative is desperately obvious to the victim. The Christian reader commiserates with the inadequacy of his faith for the required spiritual transformation even as he admires Baudelaire's moral perspicacity.

5. Les Fleurs du Mal—A history of spiritual anguish in Baudelaire's generation

Baudelaire's own evaluation of the *Poésies de Joseph Delorme* as the "*Fleurs du Mal* de la veille" and as a preparation for the spiritual history of Amaury lends validity to an attempt to compare the psychological portraits of Sainte-Beuve's two heroes with that of the complex ego which presides over the *Fleurs du Mal*. Marcel Ruff's convincing argument for the aesthetic unity of the *Fleurs*[1] suggests the advisability of examining only the two editions of this work subject to the poet's personal supervision, those of 1857 and 1861. The aesthetic evolution of the work can be traced by studying the various groups of poems as they appear before the 1857 edition: first the *Limbes* of 1851; then the *Douze poèmes* sent to Théophile Gautier in 1852; the collection of poems published in the *Revue des Deux Mondes* of June, 1855; and finally the groups published in the April, 1857, number

1. Ruff, *L'esprit du mal*, pp. 350-365. Also chaps. xxii, xxiii, xxiv, and xxv.

of the *Revue Française* and in the May, 1857, edition of *L'Artiste*. The artistic unity achieved in the first complete edition of the *Fleurs* (1857) reflects two tendencies in the poet's total psyche: a consciousness of the predominant role of evil in the spiritual destiny of man, and the awareness of an engulfing personal catastrophe which is spiritual rather than material.[2] The psychological atmosphere of the *Fleurs* is thus created around a double personality—an artist interpreting universal truth through an aesthetic of cosmic evil, and a suffering human being confounded in his own spiritual chaos. The hardships in Baudelaire's life contributed to an elegiac disposition in his artistic personality akin to that of the early Sainte-Beuve. One cannot assume that either the Delorme poems or the *Fleurs* present a completely accurate image of their author's personality, but it is clear that the life history of each poet gave an individual flavor to his interpretation of the splenetic temperament. In the case of Baudelaire, the individuality is considerably influenced by the personal suffering of the "sacrifié de la vie"[3] in his unending search for the Absolute. As for a deliberate cult of spiritual suffering, he acknowledged something of a disciple's indebtedness in verses addressed to Sainte-Beuve in 1844:

J'ai partout feuilleté le mystère profond
De ce livre si cher aux âmes engourdies
Que leur destin marqua des mêmes maladies,
Et, devant le miroir, j'ai perfectionné
L'art cruel qu'un démon, en naissant, m'a donné,
—De la douleur pour faire une volupté vraie,—
D'ensanglanter un mal et de gratter sa plaie.

In tracing the emergence of an individual psychology in the *Fleurs*, it is difficult to determine at what point the elegiac

2. Benjamin Fondane, *Baudelaire et l'expérience du gouffre* (Paris: Seghers, 1947), pp. 131-132, 328.
3. *Ibid.*, p. 165.

disposition and conscious aesthetic begin to influence traditional lyric themes inherited from earlier French Romanticists. With very few exceptions, the poetic ingredients of the *Juvenilia* (written before 1842) present problems of authenticity and collaboration which make them unsuited to a study in aesthetic direction. In the *Limbes* (1851) Marcel Ruff cautiously sketches a modest aesthetic evolution from a few earlier poems composed under specific influences to the final orderly collection[4] inspired, according to Baudelaire himself, by the spiritual anguish of contemporary youth.[5] Prarond suggested in 1886 that many more of the *Fleurs* had been composed during the early period (1842-1844) than the number later indicated by Ruff.[6] If this is so, a much more conclusive aesthetic tendency can be ascribed to the compositions of the earlier period than has been supposed. The significance attached by both Prarond and Ruff to compositions appearing before the *Limbes* of 1851 certainly justifies a brief examination of poems generally accepted as written before 1844. The aim of this survey will be to determine what early aesthetic orientation appears in Baudelaire's relatively immature poetic creation.

The early poems tend to gravitate toward one pole or the other of the dual postulation in man's soul, inasmuch as they are concerned with either the *extase* or the *horreur* of mortal life. Two of the earliest *Fleurs*, "A une dame créole," composed in 1841, and "A une Malabaraise," probably written in 1842, are characteristic of Baudelaire's exotic poetry, in which the poet tends to relate the tropical settings of the Ile Maurice to a primitive paradisiac state linked with the lost Eden of childhood.[7] The poetic re-creation of a tropical

4. Ruff, *L'esprit du mal*, pp. 244-245.
5. Charles Baudelaire, *Les Fleurs du Mal*, ed. Jacques Crépet et Georges Blin (Paris: José Corti, 1942), p. 230. See editor's note.
6. Baudelaire, *Œuvres complètes*, II, 1155. Letter from Ernest Prarond to Eugène Crépet, Oct., 1886.
7. Fondane, p. 123.

paradise joins in a wider exoticism to furnish the poet in the future with the means of escape from the *horreur* of immediate reality. The horror of physical decay is dissolved in "Une charogne" by the spiritual transfiguration of the corpse and the expression of its ideal essence in timeless poetry. The horror implicit in the enforced baseness of the under-privileged masses may be temporarily dispersed by the intoxicating power of wine, as in "L'âme du vin." In "Le vin de l'assassin" the corrosion of time has turned the *extase* of idealized passion into the *horreur* of all the sufferings inherent in the tyranny of erotic love. The evasion sought by the murderer is a mental and spiritual void, beyond the range of sentiment or morality. A similar evasion is sought in the amorality of the austere beauty evoked in "Allégorie." This formal beauty is answerable only to a law of aesthetic enjoyment for its own sake, being indifferent to the ravages of time or the excesses of debauchery. Evaluating itself as a supernatural gift, it arrogates to itself innocence of any crime inspired by it. In "J'aime le souvenir de ces époques nues" there is an antithesis between an apparent *extase* represented by the primitive harmony of the Greek golden age and the *horreur* of modern nineteenth-century civilization. The horror of modern life is of course later transfigured by poetic creation into the heroism of modernity. In "La muse malade" ecstasy is represented by an appeal for the fusion of virile Christian thought with the robust harmony of classical verse. The opposing *horreur* is represented in the morbid preoccupations of a mind ravaged by organic disease and spiritual anguish. The poem "Le soleil" is only loosely associated with the classical theme common to the three preceding poems; it does, however, reinforce the idea of dualism found in them. In addition to its physical function in nature, the sun, as creative energy, animates both the suffering Parisians and their poet. Poetic creativity ennobles "le sort des choses les plus viles" and inspires the artist to triumph over the tormenting difficulties of his art. Poetic aspiration and the common man's spiritual aspiration are fused in one harvest of the sublime.

Three poems, "Don Juan aux Enfers," "Châtiment de l'orgueil," and "Le rebelle" form a group in which, underneath conscious revolt, lies an incipient sense of guilt. In this small cycle of revolt, intellectual and moral arrogance are presented as subtle and highly dangerous elements in the *horreur* of man's life. Don Juan's cynical arrogance is merely a temporary escape from the failure of his aspirations toward the Infinite. The warning of "Châtiment de l'orgueil" appears to be uttered against the danger of egocentrism in the spiritual aspirations of the *extase*. The latter, through excessive man-centeredness, may revert to the very *horreur* which it seeks to escape. The conflict of opposing wills treated in "Le rebelle" illustrates the inability of the poet to reanimate his soul, deadened by spiritual ennui, in the *extase* of Christian charity. Finally, in "Les deux bonnes sœurs," the *horreur de la vie* is reflected in the debauchery of the flesh and in death. For Baudelaire the unfailing sequel to carnal indulgence is barren remorse. But more than remorse, the wages of sin are death, which for this sinner means the brutal extinction of the soul in the false tranquillity of a complete void.

In the *Echo des Marchands de Vin* there appeared in November, 1848, an announcement of the forthcoming publication of a group of Baudelaire's poems under the title of *Les Limbes*. Part of this group was published in *Le Messager de L'Assemblée* of April 9, 1851, with an accompanying note which declared that the object of the collection was to present a history of the anguish of modern youth, an elegy of the young generation in limbo. This declared aim lends strong support to the contention that Baudelaire's title indicates a neutral zone of Hell, equally devoid of joy or suffering; a logical habitat for lost souls in search of paradise; a location

for the soul in a state of Baudelairean spleen.[8] The eleven
poems of the *Limbes* reveal the first tendency toward a conscious aesthetic of evil suggested by the final title, *Les Fleurs
du Mal.* This dominant aesthetic and its component psychological themes become even more obvious in a collection of
twelve poems sent to Théophile Gautier in 1852 for his approval, with a view to publication in the *Revue de Paris.* In
a letter to Watripon of May, 1852,[9] Baudelaire reaffirmed
the forthcoming publication of his *Limbes,* but later in the
same month abandoned this title, probably on learning of
its previous use by another writer.

The poems from the *Limbes*[10] show certain clear thematic
divisions characterized chiefly by increasing frustration and
a deepening consciousness of personal guilt. Four compositions, "Pluviôse, irrité . . .," "Le mauvais moine," "L'Idéal,"
and "Le mort joyeux" evidence a pessimism short of despair
and tempered by the possibility of remedial or evasive action
by the poet or the man. In "Pluviôse, irrité . . ." the poet's
sordid surroundings become an objective correlative for his
personal ennui. Here the artist uses spleen to destroy that un-
pleasant reality through the creation of a poetic reality. The
ultimate consequence of ennui in this sonnet is thus a world
of reversed values, where the inanimate beings of the tercets
assume animate qualities which reflect the atmosphere of
pallid decrepitude.[11] Thus his personal suffering is assuaged
in this poetic transformation.

In "Le mauvais moine" another kind of transformation is
demanded: the dispersal through poetic creativity of the in-

8. Thibaudet, *Histoire de la littérature française,* p. 325.
9. Baudelaire, *Correspondance,* I, 171-173.
10. Baudelaire, *Fleurs,* p. 230. Crépet and Blin list the following poems:
"Pluviôse, irrité . . .," "Le mauvais moine," "L'Idéal," "Le mort joyeux," "Les
chats," "La mort des artistes," "La mort des amants," "Le tonneau de la
haine," "De profundis clamavi," "La cloche fêlée," "Les hiboux."
11. Hubert, *L'esthétique des Fleurs du Mal,* pp. 106-108.

sidious invasion of the mind by acedia.[12] Such creation should, moreover, draw its inspiration from the very misery which produces this dangerous kind of introversion. The *horreur de la vie* thus assumes in this poem the special form of the difficulties encountered in creating poetry, difficulties which are an integral part of the over-all psychology of Baudelairean spleen.

The sonnet "L'Idéal" is also deeply involved in Baudelaire's theory of art. In expressing his personal preference for a certain type of modern heroine, the poet takes a position which is especially significant when related to the essence of beauty established in a later *Fleur* of the 1861 edition, "L'hymne à la beauté." The quatrains of "L'Idéal" clearly affirm a rejection of such banal and anemic heroines as are painted by a modernist like Gavarni. By contrast, the author champions in the tercets the feminine type who, by reason of her sin, is fully engaged in the passionate drama of man's spiritual duality. This engagement is obviously at the profane pole of the ambivalence, but, because of the eternal possibility of the moral alternative in the drama, sin always holds a latent promise of the sublime—and hence of poetry. The very consciousness of evil in the poet's preference thus paradoxically promotes a remedial reaction through poetic creation which can achieve his professional redemption. As for his personal redemption, it is pertinent to add that the logic of Catholic theology has always envisaged original sin as the prologue to the Resurrection.

The last of the four poems, "Le mort joyeux," was to belong eventually to a group of three frenetic compositions which terminate the cycle of spleen in the 1857 edition of the *Fleurs*. Chérix claims that this sonnet reveals a new poetic landscape in the true cycle of ennui. In the hedonistic intoxication of

12. "Accidie," *The Oxford Dictionary of the Christian Church*, ed. F. L. Cross (London: Oxford University Press, 1957), p. 10.

death, the normally spiritual Baudelaire here acquires the soul of a nihilist. His frigid despair is warmed by the idea of total oblivion, in which both self and the world of men are dissolved.[13]

There is no clearly indicated group of the *Limbes* to which the poem "Les chats" may be satisfactorily joined, but, because of its evocative power, it might be related to the foregoing four poems.[14] These feline creatures, chosen by Baudelaire above all others as the symbol of his own complex psyche, possess qualities of languor and inscrutability which reflect his splenetic moods. Whether he be a frustrated artist or a prey to erotic passion, they are the preferred projection of his own ego.

In the mounting *horreur de la vie* which tears at the poet's very soul, death, by terminating the physical existence, provides an escape, at least from the torments of terrestrial reality. Within the important cycle of poems on death, "La mort des artistes" depicts the pains of artistic creation. The relentless pursuit of the elusive poetic ideal exhausts the spirit, without any assurance that the poet will attain his sublime objective. For those artists who are denied the fruition of their genius in the earthly life, there remains only the hope that in the life beyond the grave they will receive the divine illumination of artistic truth:

Il en est qui jamais n'ont connu leur Idole,
Et ces sculpteurs damnés et marqués d'un affront,
Qui vont se martelant la poitrine et le front,

N'ont qu'un espoir, étrange et sombre Capitole!
C'est que la Mort, planant comme un Soleil nouveau,
Fera s'épanouir les fleurs de leur cerveau!

The other *Limbe* in the cycle of death, "La mort des amants," foretells the sublimation of imperfect worldly love

13. Chérix, *Commentaire des Fleurs du Mal*, pp. 262-263.
14. Ruff, *L'esprit du mal*, p. 245.

between man and woman. The almost exotic richness of the first quatrain in this sonnet provides the setting for a transfiguration which begins even in the last phase of worldly love. In the second quatrain the ardor of erotic passion is transformed into an incandescent spirituality at the approach of death. The eventual mystical union of two souls is presented in the final tercet:

> Et plus tard un Ange, entr'ouvrant les portes,
> Viendra ranimer, fidèle et joyeux,
> Les miroirs ternis et les flammes mortes.

Retaliating blindly against the encircling evils of the worldly life, the splenetic type develops an unquenchable thirst for vengeance. This spirit of revenge, announced in "Le tonneau de la haine," is clearly essential to the group of spleen poems which follow in the edition of 1857. Since it cannot be sated, hate prolongs by its restless vigilance the very *horreur* in which it is born, rejecting more and more the possibility of the *extase*.

A discouragement more personal and profound than expressed hitherto is apparent in two sonnets which are part of the cycle of spleen in the *Limbes*. In the first of these, "De profundis clamavi," is described the frigid desolation of moral and spiritual decadence. The lover of Jeanne Duval makes an unusual and probably futile appeal to the spiritual pole of his mistress' nature. The second quatrain of the sonnet suggests that the spiritual abyss enveloping the poet has its origin in the remorse which follows the sterility of carnal passion. The second of the two sonnets, "La cloche fêlée," describes a morbid despair, in which the source of spleen is artistic sterility. In contrast with the creative vigor of the "cloche alerte et bien portante," the futile efforts of the poet fail to respond to the poetic suggestivity of the "souvenirs lointains" evoked in the first quatrain:

Moi, mon âme est fêlée, et lorsqu'en ses ennuis
Elle veut de ses chants peupler l'air froid des nuits,
Il arrive souvent que sa voix affaiblie

Semble le râle épais d'un blessé qu'on oublie
Au bord d'un lac de sang, sous un grand tas de morts,
Et qui meurt sans bouger dans d'immenses efforts.

The concluding poem in the 1851 series of *Limbes*, "Les hiboux," restates an ageless lesson of Pascal on the vanity of diversion. Hubert's commentary on this lesson seems, with its theological emphasis, highly significant for any examination of the bipolarity in Baudelaire's psychology. Proceeding from the conception of a fusion of moral and physical attitudes, he notes that the tumult and movement in which man changes his location and which prevent meditation and contemplation carry within themselves the seeds of anguish. The desire of Adam for a situation different from that given him by God caused original sin, which became an eternal punishment for human posterity.[15] Baudelaire's escape from the *horreur* and attainment of the *extase* were too frequently a resort to artificial paradises, which resulted only in new pangs of remorse and ennui. The discovery of the sublime within the very conditions of the worldly life would have been the solution to the poet's grave dilemma. In the personal sphere, this discovery was denied him. Only in poetic creation did he come to know something of the ecstasy in God's universe.

Baudelaire drew further upon his *Limbes*, developing the dominant aesthetic of the collection progressively, in the *Douze poèmes* sent to Théophile Gautier in 1852.[16] At the

15. Hubert, pp. 115-117.
16. The *Douze poèmes* of 1852 included the following: "Le crépuscule du soir," "Le crépuscule du matin," "A une mendiante rousse," "La rançon," "Le vin des chiffonniers," "La mort des pauvres," "Le reniement de saint Pierre," "Bohémiens en voyage," "Les métamorphoses du vampire," "La fontaine de sang," "Un voyage à Cythère," "Le guignon."

beginning of this second series, the emphasis falls upon the anonymous observation of evil erupting in the metropolis. It subsequently shifts in the course of this same series to the confession of personal experience in evil, experience nevertheless endowed with universal significance. The first of two Parisian poems is "Le crépuscule du soir." Here night is briefly introduced as the accomplice of all that is sinful in the life of the city's inhabitants:

> Voici le soir charmant, ami du criminel;
> Il vient comme un complice, à pas de loup; le ciel
> Se ferme lentement comme une grande alcôve,
> Et l'homme impatient se change en bête fauve.

In the second strophe of the poem, evening is characterized as the solace of a day's labor well done:

> O soir, aimable soir, désiré par celui
> Dont les bras, sans mentir, peuvent dire: Aujourd'hui
> Nous avons travaillé!—C'est le soir qui soulage
> Les esprits que dévore une douleur sauvage,
> Le savant obstiné dont le front s'alourdit,
> Et l'ouvrier courbé qui regagne son lit.

The false pleasure of the innumerable vices produced by the demonic animation described in the third strophe is concealed in the nocturnal darkness:

> Cependant des démons malsains dans l'atmosphère
> S'éveillent lourdement, comme des gens d'affaire,
> Et cognent en volant les volets et l'auvent.
> A travers les lueurs que tourmente le vent
> La Prostitution s'allume dans les rues;
> Comme une fourmilière elle ouvre ses issues;
> Partout elle se fraye un occulte chemin,
> Ainsi que l'ennemi qui tente un coup de main;
> Elle remue au sein de la cité de fange
> Comme un ver qui dérobe à l'Homme ce qu'il mange.

The defensive introversion of the poet-observer cannot escape the sinister roar of nocturnal evil, to which, in the fourth strophe, is added the plaint of relatively innocent suffering:

C'est l'heure où les douleurs des malades s'aigrissent!
La sombre Nuit les prend à la gorge; ils finissent
Leur destinée et vont vers le gouffre commun;
L'hôpital se remplit de leurs soupirs.—Plus d'un
Ne viendra plus chercher la soupe parfumée,
Au coin du feu, le soir, auprès d'une âme aimée.

The second Parisian poem, "Le crépuscule du matin," depicts in three stages the awakening of the metropolis and of its inhabitants. First, the dawning day draws from slumber the citizen's cantankerous and heavy body, in which a struggling conscience is troubled by malevolent dreams. In the second stage of the poem, the author-observer evokes sufferings other than his own: for example, the torpor of the noctambulists and the sleeplessness of the bedridden. The third stage describes the awakening of the city to another day of labor. These three stages provide an almost symmetrical inversion of the motifs apparent in the preceding poem, "Le crépuscule du soir."

Baudelaire presents in "A une mendiante rousse" a street scene in which a young mendicant entertainer becomes the symbol of a beauty which triumphs over both poverty and vice. In the 1861 edition of the *Fleurs*, the figure of the "mendiante rousse" appears on the threshold of the "Tableaux parisiens," which are dedicated to the tragic drama of metropolitan existence. The commiserative tone of the Parisian poems is also apparent in "La rançon." This didactic work, which will not reappear until the 1868 edition of the *Fleurs*, has as its theme the co-operation of artistic creation and Christian charity in establishing conditions favorable to the poet's salvation on the day of divine judgment.

A blend of idealism and sordid realism similar to that of "A une mendiante rousse" appears in "Le vin des chiffonniers." This poem, although it will appear in the 1857 edition under the cycle of wine, is by its compassionate tone appropriate to the cycle of observed external suffering. In the 1852 version, the imagination of a base ragpicker encountered in the streets of Paris assumes, under alcoholic stimulation, the magic felicity of a universal enchantment. Over the features of this veteran of Bonaparte's armies are superimposed those of an idiot full of humanitarian virtue. The same tone of compassion, together with the promise of ultimate consolation for all worldly suffering, appears in the sonnet "La mort des pauvres," although in the 1857 edition this poem will be formally assigned to the cycle of death. In this composition death is shown as the sole gateway to an *extase* which is impossible in the terrestrial existence of the poor.

Man's protest against the oppressive conditions of his earthly life finds expression in the poem "Le reniement de saint Pierre." God the Creator is here revealed as indifferent to his creation:

> Qu'est-ce que Dieu fait donc de ce flot d'anathèmes
> Qui monte tous les jours vers ses chers Séraphins?
> Comme un tyran gorgé de viande et de vins,
> Il s'endort au doux bruit de nos affreux blasphèmes.
>
> Les sanglots des martyrs et des suppliciés
> Sont une symphonie enivrante sans doute,
> Puisque, malgré le sang que leur volupté coûte,
> Les cieux ne s'en sont point encore rassasiés!

Jesus Christ is made in his Passion to symbolize the frustration of man's sublime aspirations:

> Quand de ton corps brisé la pesanteur horrible
> Allongeait tes deux bras distendus, que ton sang

Et ta sueur coulaient de ton front pâlissant,
Quand tu fus devant tous posé comme une cible,

Rêvais-tu de ces jours si brillants et si beaux
Où tu vins pour remplir l'éternelle promesse,
Où tu foulais, monté sur une douce ânesse,
Des chemins tout jonchés de fleurs et de rameaux,

Où, le cœur tout gonflé d'espoir et de vaillance,
Tu fouettais tous ces vils marchands à tour de bras,
Où tu fus maître enfin? Le remords n'a-t-il pas
Pénétré dans ton flanc plus avant que la lance?

"Un monde où l'action n'est pas la sœur du rêve" clearly figures the antithesis between spleen and ideal—between the *horreur* and the *extase*—which is fundamental in the division of man's soul. In stating what is after all basic to the spiritual anguish of any generation, Baudelaire was true to the aesthetic purpose which he claimed for his *Limbes* in 1851. As "le pastiche des raisonnements de l'ignorance et de la fureur," this poem occupies an effective position in the spiritual pattern of the *Douze poèmes*.

In the collection of 1852 sent to Gautier, "Bohémiens en voyage" is the last of the group of eight compositions in which the note of despair is relatively restrained. According to Ruff's highly plausible interpretation, this sonnet symbolizes the destiny of the artist, who is dedicated to a noble wretchedness, to a nomadic and precarious life, but who is also endowed with a divine privilege.[17] Hubert confirms Ruff's opinion, contending that the gypsies' journey represents the poetic soul in search of the poem confusedly perceived by his artistic genius.[18]

A group of three poems that follows evidences a candid confrontation of acute evil. In these several encounters, it

17. Ruff, *L'esprit du mal*, p. 250.
18. Hubert, pp. 164-165.

becomes necessary to dissolve the *horreur de la vie* in its guise of *extase*. The process of dissolution does not, however, create a true ecstasy to fill the resulting void. This spiritual vacuum thus becomes the source of permanent anguish for the poet. In the first of the three poems, "Les métamorphoses du vampire," Baudelaire delivers a powerful denunciation of carnal love as an artificial and deceptive paradise. His purpose is achieved in part by assigning to the temptress herself the normally male initiative:

—"Moi, j'ai la lèvre humide, et je sais la science
De perdre au fond d'un lit l'antique conscience.
Je sèche tous les pleurs sur mes seins triomphants,
Et fais rire les vieux du rire des enfants.
Je remplace, pour qui me voit nue et sans voiles,
La lune, le soleil, le ciel et les étoiles!
Je suis, mon cher savant, si docte aux voluptés,
Lorsque j'étouffe un homme en mes bras redoutés,
Ou lorsque j'abandonne aux morsures mon buste,
Timide et libertine, et fragile et robuste,
Que sur ces matelas qui se pâment d'émoi,
Les anges impuissants se damneraient pour moi!"

Remaining a passive victim in the first part of the poem, the poet-lover speaks only after the paroxysm of the love act, as physical passion rapidly fades and finally vanishes:

Je fermai les deux yeux, dans ma froide épouvante,
Et quand je les rouvris à la clarté vivante,
A mes côtés, au lieu du mannequin puissant
Qui semblait avoir fait provision de sang,
Tremblaient confusément des débris de squelette,
Qui d'eux-mêmes rendaient le cri d'une girouette
Ou d'une enseigne, au bout d'une tringle de fer,
Que balance le vent pendant les nuits d'hiver.

The erotic contortions of carnal seduction in the first part of the poem become in the second division the oscillations of the conscience, of which the weather vane is the symbol.

The ultimate insolvency of the "paradis artificiels," especially those procured through carnal love or the "vins captieux," is announced in the acute despair of the sonnet "La fontaine de sang." The relentless draining of physical and spiritual forces in the indulgence of the senses is the persistent reality confronted in this poem.

The most powerful confession of the sterility of carnal love is found in the last composition of the group, "Un voyage à Cythère." The poet's journey to the isle of Venus, although presented in spatial terms, in fact symbolizes his enthusiastic approach to the false paradise of passion. The putrified corpse on its "gibet à trois branches" which greets the hopeful traveler clearly represents Baudelaire's disillusionment with the temptations of the flesh. The symbolic "gibet" recalls in the poet's memory the bitter fruits of his erotic past. In his present spiritual lucidity he is appalled by the reality of his earlier engagement in the "infâmes cultes" of Venus.

Last in the series, "Le guignon" features the anguish of poetic creation. The elusiveness of inspiration and the brevity of the poet's life expectancy are weighed against his professional courage. In the tercets of this sonnet, creative impotence is seen as the result of his failure to probe the depths of his own subconscious:

> —Maint joyau dort enseveli
> Dans les ténèbres et l'oubli,
> Bien loin des pioches et des sondes;
>
> Mainte fleur épanche à regret
> Son parfum doux comme un secret
> Dans les solitudes profondes.

The failure described in this particular poem is one of several contributing to its author's general feeling of insufficiency. It was certainly the one most difficult for him to accept, for he placed tenacious faith in poetry as the only remaining link with his lost ideal paradise.

In the foregoing twenty-two *Limbes* the spiritual dilemma of modern youth is mirrored in the individual psychology of the poet himself. The seeming blasphemy of "Le reniement de saint Pierre" defines this personal anguish as a sense of the inadequacy of earthly existence for man's highest aspirations. This insufficiency derives from grave disappointments in artistic creation and in erotic passion, to which is added a feeling of compassion for the multiple sufferings of the Parisian populace. The present life holds no promise of rectification for any of these deficiencies, but it is suggested in the cycle of death that in eternal life art, love, and poverty may be redeemed. The future orientation of the *Fleurs du Mal* is foreshadowed in these two series by the poet's conscious engagement in the universal drama of spiritual ambivalence. This engagement at the heart of the contemporary anxiety forms the basis of modern heroism in Baudelaire's poetry.

From 1852, when he abandoned the title *Limbes*, until 1855, Baudelaire did not adopt any title for his collected poems. In October, 1852, he published "L'homme et la mer," in which he drew an analogy between his own psyche and the sea as a symbol of depth and bitterness. The title of *Fleurs du Mal* was first given to the poems appearing in the *Revue des Deux Mondes* in 1855.[19] This collection showed its author in a deeply serious mood, obsessed with the satanic presence of evil in his own earthly life and in that of universal man. He appears conscious that the most lethal metamorphosis of the satanic temptation is in the spiritual vacuum, in the ennui which engulfs him personally, paralyzing his aspirations

19. The *Fleurs* published in 1855 include the following poems: "Au lecteur," "L'ennemi," "La destruction," "Le vampire," "L'amour et le crâne," "Remords posthume," "Réversibilité," "Confession," "L'aube spirituelle," "L'irréparable," "L'invitation au voyage," "Moesta et errabunda," "La vie antérieure."

toward the Infinite. Yet the almost total pessimism of these poems drives the author to a serious examination of his conscience rather than to sheer despair. The high spirituality of the compositions includes a note of humble contrition. The prefatory poem of the series, "Au lecteur," portrays the most frightful of the beasts inhabiting the infamous menagerie of man's sins, spleen—that mortal tedium vitae which is the most accomplished form of Satan's seduction. The essence of this temptation is the invitation to non-participation in life.[20] The process of splenetic decay will become a prominent subject for Baudelaire's psychological observation, in relation both to himself and to universal man. In the same tone, the sonnet entitled "L'ennemi" implies a moral leprosy by which life secretly but inexorably withers away. The enemy is presumably to be identified with satanic ennui.

As in the *Limbes*, one of the most prolific sources of ennui is carnal desire and the disenchantment which follows its consummation. In the 1855 collection of *Fleurs* a group of three poems is devoted to the sins of the flesh. A particularly dense analysis of this sin is made in the first of the poems, "La destruction." This sonnet recounts the progressive advances of Satan: his skilful adoption of the seductive disguise of womanly beauty in artistic form and his deceptive adroitness in accustoming the sinner to his sin:

> Parfois il prend, sachant mon grand amour de l'Art,
> La forme de la plus séduisante des femmes,
> Et, sous de spécieux prétextes de cafard,
> Accoutume ma lèvre à des philtres infâmes.

The Devil's whispered temptations, with their enchanted air of magic potions, prove to be an illusion which contrasts cruelly with the disenchantment of the sinner's remorse:

20. Fondane, p. 328.

Il me conduit ainsi, loin du regard de Dieu,
Haletant et brisé de fatigue, au milieu
Des plaines de l'Ennui, profondes et désertes,

Et jette dans mes yeux pleins de confusion
Des vêtements souillés, des blessures ouvertes,
Et l'appareil sanglant de la Destruction.

The second poem, "Le vampire," has as its theme the progressive weakening of the will which inevitably results from the enslaving passions of the flesh. His curse upon his mistress in the first half of the poem suggests that he envisages a release from erotic slavery in murder. However, so powerful is the domination of profane love that the malediction and its accompanying dream of freedom are transformed in the second part into a declaration of renewed submission and loyalty. The third poem of this group, "L'amour et le crâne," describes the destruction of the human substance by the corrosion of carnal passion. The sonnet "Remords posthume" is indirectly related to this group by the implied rebuke of the mulatto mistress for wantonness, which has wasted the opportunities of a more sublime love.

A need for some escape from the remorse of the flesh led to Baudelaire's astonishing cult of Apollonie Sabatier and to the cycle of highly spiritual poems dedicated to her. To this cycle of the "Vénus blanche" belong three compositions in the *Fleurs* of 1855. The first, "Réversibilité," actually sent under anonymous cover to Madame Sabatier in May, 1853, furnishes a poignant contrast between the inadequacy of the poet's own existence and what appears to him as Apollonie's angelic sufficiency:

Ange plein de gaieté, connaissez-vous l'angoisse,
La honte, les remords, les sanglots, les ennuis,
Et les vagues terreurs de ces affreuses nuits
Qui compriment le cœur comme un papier qu'on froisse?

.   .   .   .

Ange plein de bonté, connaissez-vous la haine,
Les poings crispés dans l'ombre et les larmes de fiel,
Quand la Vengeance bat son infernal rappel,
Et de nos facultés se fait le capitaine?

.   .   .   .

Ange plein de beauté, connaissez-vous les rides,
Et la peur de vieillir, et ce hideux tourment
De lire la secrète horreur du dévouement
Dans des yeux où longtemps burent nos yeux avides?

The poet's agonized interrogation is transformed in the final
strophe into a prayer for the intercession of the beloved:

Ange plein de bonheur, de joie et de lumières,
David mourant aurait demandé la santé
Aux emanations de ton corps enchanté;
Mais de toi je n'implore, ange, que tes prières,
Ange plein de bonheur, de joie et de lumières!

The second poem, "Confession," similarly dedicated in 1853,
reiterates the theme of transience in earthly values. The cruel
ravage of time creates the elegiac element in the mortal his-
tories of love and beauty. The egoism of the human heart is
seen to be a precarious foundation on which to build the hopes
of terrestrial happiness. The third poem, "L'aube spirituelle,"
sent to Madame Sabatier in February, 1854, emphasizes the
dual postulation in man's soul, the conflict waged there between angel and beast. As for Baudelaire's personal anguish,
Apollonie beckons him at the sublime pole of his spiritual
duality:

Sur les débris fumeux des stupides orgies
Ton souvenir plus clair, plus rose, plus charmant,
A mes yeux agrandis voltige incessamment.

Le soleil a noirci la flamme des bougies;
Ainsi, toujours vainqueur, ton fantôme est pareil,
Ame resplendissante, à l'immortel soleil!

The poem "L'irréparable," while not belonging to the cycle of the "Vénus blanche," can properly be related to the series on spiritual love. Baudelaire uses here a group of varied and not very clearly linked symbols to illustrate the psychological complexity of remorse. The source of these images appears to be the dramatic fairy tale *La belle aux cheveux d'or*, produced at the Porte Saint-Martin Theatre in 1847 and featuring the poet's onetime mistress, Marie Daubrun.[21] In this composition the dissolution of spiritual petrifaction is sought through the compassionate love of a being who brings a message of redemption. Assuming that the poem was indeed addressed to Marie Daubrun, one may question whether that lady was worthy of such a grave spiritual trust.

The cult of Apollonie Sabatier, and to some extent of Marie Daubrun, as sources of comfort for the soul offered Baudelaire temporary escape from immediate reality. But the resuscitation, even by Christian intercession, of spirituality was too dependent on personal factors to provide any permanent cure for the poet's extreme ennui. Reasons for this inadequacy may be found in the very nature of Baudelaire's spiritual agony as it is most convincingly described by Benjamin Fondane in his *Baudelaire et l'expérience du gouffre*. To escape from the crushing despair of universal evil and personal spleen, the soul in perpetual search of evasion is drawn constantly toward a paradise of innocence and childlike purity. Fondane explains this nostalgia for an idealized childhood in terms of an absolute adherence to a world in which emotion, untroubled by knowledge of the Freudian principle of reality, controls the heart.[22] The same phenomenon is elsewhere described as "la

21. Baudelaire, *Fleurs*, pp. 391-392.
22. Fondane, p. 164.

nostalgie de l'arrière-monde."[23] This desire for a lost paradise inspires in the *Fleurs* of 1855 a small group of poems devoted to exotic evasion. In the first of these, "L'invitation au voyage," the pressing need to escape is expressed in a yearning for places half-remembered, half-imagined. The country envisaged in the poet's dream is bathed in an atmosphere identifiable with the nature of the poet's feeling for Marie Daubrun. It offers a landscape reflecting her calm sweetness of disposition and an equilibrium suited to an affection without violence and perhaps without strong sensual passion:

> Mon enfant, ma sœur,
> Songe à la douceur
> D'aller là-bas vivre ensemble!
> Aimer à loisir,
> Aimer et mourir
> Au pays qui te ressemble!
> Les soleils mouillés
> De ces ciels brouillés
> Pour mon esprit ont les charmes
> Si mystérieux
> De tes traîtres yeux,
> Brillant à travers leurs larmes.
>
> Là, tout n'est qu'ordre et beauté,
> Luxe, calme et volupté.

A return to the absolute realm of childlike purity which is anterior to the corrupting fruits of knowledge understood as the secular logos is the theme of the second poem in the group, "Moesta et errabunda." The poet is eager to flee the "noir océan de l'immonde cité" for another, where "la splendeur éclate, bleu, clair, profond, ainsi que la virginité":

> Emporte-moi, wagon! enlève-moi, frégate!
> Loin! Loin! ici la boue est faite de nos pleurs!

23. Georges Blin, *Baudelaire* (Paris: Gallimard, 1939), p. 103.

—Est-il vrai que parfois le triste cœur d'Agathe
Dise: Loin des remords, des crimes, des douleurs,
Emporte-moi, wagon, enlève-moi, frégate?

Comme vous êtes loin, paradis parfumé,
Où sous un clair azur tout n'est qu'amour et joie,
Où tout ce que l'on aime est digne d'être aimé,
Où dans la volupté pure le cœur se noie!
Comme vous êtes loin, paradis parfumé!

Last of the three poems, "La vie antérieure" likewise treats the theme of escape from immediate reality, be it a return to the absolute of a childhood paradise or to some pre-existence suggested by palingenetic philosophy. Whatever may be the occult significance of the "vastes portiques" and the "grottes basaltiques" in this sonnet, the veil of mystery is not lifted in the text. What is specifically stated is that the calm ecstasy of a tropical environment is capable of submerging in oblivion a secret anguish which is undermining the poet's very being.

The spiritual itinerary of Baudelaire continues in a group of *Fleurs* published in the *Revue Française* of April, 1857.[24] While this series does not strongly emphasize the poet's pessimism, the several poems relate to particular attitudes in his aesthetic or moral outlook which are connected with his spiritual dilemma. The sonnet "La géante" is the first of three compositions devoted simply to aesthetic concepts. Chérix and Ruff agree in interpreting this work as a plastic stylization reflecting Baudelaire's own preference for the bizarre dimension in art.[25] These coinciding views are certainly supported by the poet's own evaluation of a prodigious statue by Clésinger.[26]

24. The *Fleurs* published in the *Revue Française* of April, 1857, include the following: "La géante," "La Beauté," "Avec ses vêtements ondoyants et nacrés," "Le flambeau vivant," "Tout entière," "Harmonie du soir," "Le flacon," "Je te donne ces vers," "Le poison."
25. Chérix, p. 91; Marcel A. Ruff, "Notules Baudelairiennes," *Revue d'Histoire littéraire de la France*, 51e année (1951), pp. 483-486.
26. Baudelaire, "Salon de 1859," *Œuvres complètes*, II, 154.

Prarond sets the date for this poem as 1843, and the appearance of this unconventional taste in dimension in so early a composition is hardly surprising. The second poem of the group, "La Beauté," affirms the impassive transcendence of art:

Je suis belle, ô mortels! comme un rêve de pierre,
Et mon sein, où chacun s'est meurtri tour à tour,
Est fait pour inspirer au poète un amour
Eternel et muet ainsi que la matière.

Je trône dans l'azur comme un sphinx incompris;
J'unis un cœur de neige à la blancheur des cygnes;
Je hais le mouvement qui déplace les lignes,
Et jamais je ne pleure et jamais je ne ris.

If the emotional and moral detachment of this Beauty be compared with the spiritual engagement of Baudelaire's preferred heroine in "L'Idéal," doubt must arise as to whether the aesthetic creed expressed in the present sonnet is really suited to Baudelaire's own nature or to the moral significance of the *Fleurs du Mal.* A similarly Parnassian conception of art appears, nevertheless, in the third poem of the group, "Avec ses vêtements ondoyants et nacrés," probably inspired by Jeanne Duval:

Comme le sable morne et l'azur des déserts,
Insensibles tous deux à l'humaine souffrance,
Comme les longs réseaux de la houle des mers,
Elle se développe avec indifférence.

Ses yeux polis sont faits de minéraux charmants,
Et dans cette nature étrange et symbolique
Où l'ange inviolé se mêle au sphinx antique,

Où tout n'est qu'or, acier, lumière et diamants,
Resplendit à jamais, comme un astre inutile,
La froide majesté de la femme stérile.

Among these *Fleurs* of April, 1857, certain poems, inspired by or dedicated to Madame Sabatier, show Baudelaire's concern with the possibility of regaining religious faith and attaining spiritual salvation. In the sonnet "Le flambeau vivant," the beloved plays the role not of cruel temptress, nor even of indifferent sphinx, but of spiritual guide and comforter:

> Ils marchent devant moi, ces Yeux pleins de lumières,
> Qu'un Ange très-savant a sans doute aimantés;
> Ils marchent, ces divins frères qui sont mes frères,
> Secouant dans mes yeux leurs feux diamantés.
>
> Me sauvant de tout piège et de tout péché grave,
> Ils conduisent mes pas dans la route du Beau;
> Ils sont mes serviteurs et je suis leur esclave;
> Tout mon être obéit à ce vivant flambeau.

The poem "Tout entière" emphasizes the domination of the metaphysical image. The poet declines Satan's invitation to exalt certain parts of Apollonie's person at the expense of the whole. Such an "impuissante analyse" would only confirm the empire of merely profane passion. His acceptance rather of the harmonious whole marks the evaporation of satanic sensuality and its replacement by the mystical *volupté* of the spirit.

Two other *Fleurs* in this series of April, 1857, which are generally accepted as belonging to the cycle of Madame Sabatier, project into the past a love which had not yet come to an end.[27] In the first of these two compositions, the celebrated "Harmonie du soir," the intoxicating suggestivity of a summer evening evokes in the poet's suffering heart the memory of a "passé lumineux"—the mystical inspiration of Apollonie's beauty and affection:

> Le violon frémit comme un cœur qu'on afflige,
> Un cœur tendre, qui hait le néant vaste et noir!

27. Ruff, *L'esprit du mal*, p. 301.

Le ciel est triste et beau comme un grand reposoir;
Le soleil s'est noyé dans son sang qui se fige.

Un cœur tendre, qui hait le néant vaste et noir,
Du passé lumineux recueille tout vestige!
Le soleil s'est noyé dans son sang qui se fige . . .
Ton souvenir en moi luit comme un ostensoir!

The other projection of love into the past is effected in "Le flacon." In this poem the memory of his bittersweet love for the "Vénus blanche" is activated in the depths of the poet's despair by a chance perfume:

Voilà le souvenir enivrant qui voltige
Dans l'air troublé; les yeux se ferment; le Vertige
Saisit l'âme vaincue et la pousse à deux mains
Vers un gouffre obscurci de miasmes humains;

Il la terrasse au bord d'un gouffre séculaire,
Où, Lazare odorant déchirant son suaire,
Se meut dans son réveil le cadavre spectral
D'un vieil amour ranci, charmant et sépulcral.

In a reversal of his role, the poet appears in the second part of the poem to offer by his poetry a permanent monument to a love which had both exalted and lacerated his heart:

Ainsi, quand je serai perdu dans la mémoire
Des hommes, dans le coin d'une sinistre armoire
Quand on m'aura jeté, vieux flacon désolé,
Décrépit, poudreux, sale, abject, visqueux, fêlé,

Je serai ton cercueil, aimable pestilence!
Le témoin de ta force et de ta virulence,
Cher poison préparé par les anges! liqueur
Qui me ronge, ô la vie et la mort de mon cœur!

The immortalization of the beloved in the poet's creation is also the theme of the sonnet "Je te donne ces vers," though this poem is inspired not by Madame Sabatier but by Jeanne Duval. Baudelaire's most frequent partner in the profane diversions of carnal love is invested here with a certain spirituality through the purifying mediation of art. Viewed in this light, the sonnet is made (in the 1868 edition of the *Fleurs*) to close—and quite effectively—the cycle of the "Vénus noire."

Last of the *Fleurs* published in the *Revue Française* of April, 1857, "Le poison" has little relation to the spirituality that characterizes this series as a whole. Belonging to the cycle of Marie Daubrun, the poem emphasizes the virulent corruption of the human spirit by carnal passion. The physical charms of the mistress are found superior to the artificial paradises of wine and opium:

> Tout cela ne vaut pas le poison qui découle
> De tes yeux, de tes yeux verts,
> Lacs où mon âme tremble et se voit à l'envers;
> —Mes songes viennent en foule
> Pour se désaltérer à ces gouffres amers.

In *L'Artiste* of May, 1857, were published three of Baudelaire's *Fleurs* which in their several ways express an acute consciousness of sin. In the first of these poems, "L'héautontimorouménos," an impersonal sadism directed against the poet's partner in love is balanced against the lover's sense of being himself the victim of that torture. The sadistic act is devoid of anger, because the perpetrator is aware of the psychological irony in his own spiritual duality. The remorse inspired by the suffering of the mistress is a nourishment necessary to the perverse exaltation of conscious evil. This form of self-indulgence is a poison which gradually destroys the spiritual fiber of the ironist, with the result that he becomes incapable of transforming mere remorse into repentance by a healthy application of his moral willpower. The absence of this aspiration to repentance appears to be at the heart of the "faux accord dans la divine symphonie" mentioned in the fourth stanza of the poem.

The theme of moral consciousness in the very perpetration of evil is pursued in the second poem of the group, "L'irrémédiable." The spiritual anguish of the poet—"un Etre/ Parti de l'azur et tombé/ Dans un Styx bourbeux et plombé"—engulfed in sin is represented by the allegorical emblems of the first seven stanzas. These pictures are linked by the eighth stanza, which gives a hint of the moral block achieved by the machinations of Satan, with the second part of the poem, in which consciousness of evil is revealed as a source of comfort and pride:

> —Emblèmes nets, tableau parfait
> D'une fortune irrémédiable,
> Qui donne à penser que le Diable
> Fait toujours bien tout ce qu'il fait!

II

> Tête-à-tête sombre et limpide
> Qu'un cœur devenu son miroir!
> Puits de Vérité, clair et noir,
> Où tremble une étoile livide,
>
> Un phare ironique, infernal,
> Flambeau des grâces sataniques,
> Soulagement et gloire uniques,
> —La conscience dans le Mal!

Alternating light and darkness form a paradox in the moral dialogue between the guilty conscience and the soul addicted to evil. As in the preceding poem, there is no suggestion in this composition that the ironist has yet recognized the moral alternative.

In contrast to the pessimism of the two foregoing poems, Baudelaire invokes in the last work of this series, "Franciscae meae laudes," a purifying love, a promise of redemption after so much sin, the image in reverse of the inn in "L'irréparable," where the light was extinguished by Satan:

> Quod erat spurcum, cremasti:
> Quod rudius, exaequasti;
> Quod debile, confirmasti!
> In fame mea taberna,
> In nocte mea lucerna,
> Recte me semper guberna.

The *Fleurs* of the 1857 edition which did not enjoy prior publication are grouped according to a now increasingly apparent psychological bipolarity. It embraces at one pole the *horreur de la vie* and the escape from it through artificial paradises. The other pole represents the *extase de la vie* and its projection into the supernatural, resulting from the artist's transcendental flight toward the Ideal. This very projection is the theme of a series of poems that substantially define Baudelaire's poetics. First in this group, according to the published sequence of the 1857 edition, is "Bénédiction." Baudelaire is here concerned with both the worldly and the supernatural destiny of the poet. The former is described in terms of the struggle between the artist's idealism and the moral decadence of society. In his earthly aspect, the poet is a victim of the personal suffering necessarily resulting from such a struggle. In this context the *horreur* appears as the ignorant hostility of the vulgar crowd in conflict with divine inspiration—the *extase*—in the divinely elected soul of the artist. The nature of this divine election is specified in the sixteenth stanza of the poem:

> Je sais que vous gardez une place au poète
> Dans les rangs bienheureux des saintes Légions,
> Et que vous l'invitez à l'éternelle fête
> Des Trônes, des Vertus, des Dominations.

Seeing in this poem a parody of the Immaculate Conception, Hubert emphasizes the ambiguity between the person of the poet and that of the crucified Jesus. Apart from the Romantic tradition of the persecuted artist, the poet represents also absolute art, beauty, the Ideal, and even divine creation. Like Jesus, the poet pursues the weary but triumphant way of the Cross, securing man's salvation from his own animal vulgarity by the redemptive reversibility of personal suffering and its sublimation in poetry.[28] The purifying function of worldly suffering and the relation of the purification to the supernatural life are expounded in the fifteenth stanza:

> Soyez béni, mon Dieu, qui donnez la souffrance
> Comme un divin remède à nos impuretés,
> Et comme la meilleure et la plus pure essence
> Qui prépare les forts aux saintes voluptés!

The martyr of the poetic vocation elaborated in this poem will be crowned in glory with "ce beau diadème éblouissant et clair," the pure light of which is drawn from the sacred rays of an original innocence subsequently profaned by Adam's expulsion from Eden. In all their splendor, the eyes of mortals are no more than a clouded and sad reflection of this supernatural light. In his missionary role, the poet appears to pass through an intermediate and worldly stage of the *extase de la vie* on his way to reunion with the absolute purity of the transcendental essence.

Reinforcing the theme of spirituality, "Elévation" sounds a note of the purest idealism, and this transport of the soul occurs in several subsequent *Fleurs*. In this poem the almost physical upsurge of the poet is equated with spiritual profundity. Poetic imagination achieves both an escape from mundane ennui and a translation into the absolute purity of the infinite:

28. Hubert, pp. 221-227.

Envole-toi bien loin de ces miasmes morbides;
Va te purifier dans l'air supérieur,
Et bois, comme une pure et divine liqueur,
Le feu clair qui remplit les espaces limpides.

Derrière les ennuis et les vastes chagrins
Qui chargent de leur poids l'existence brumeuse,
Heureux celui qui peut d'une aile vigoureuse
S'élancer vers les champs lumineux et sereins;

There is an important correspondence between the first line quoted from this composition and the verses addressed by Baudelaire to Sainte-Beuve in 1844. The admirer of Amaury, prepared and matured by the poetry of Joseph Delorme, cites the "miasmes" which permeate the novel *Volupté*. In both of these contexts this noun clearly connotes the splenetic element of the *horreur de la vie*.

Expressions such as "les champs lumineux et sereins" and "le langage des fleurs et des choses muettes," which symbolize absolute poetic reality in "Elévation," presage the mystical symbolism of the next poem in order, "Correspondances." The first quatrain of this sonnet is concerned with the absolute reality of the divine unity in terms of *la symbolique*—the system of symbol which relates the finite to the infinite. The created universe results from the fragmentation of infinite perfection into a multitude of finite perfections, which reflect the Ideal and are also related to each other. The symbols of nature are familiar to man because of his own conception in the image of God. The second quatrain and the tercets are concerned with *le symbolisme*—the interrelationship between the fragments of divine perfection through a synesthesia of the sense impressions. *Symbolisme* is obviously important for the creation of poetic images, but the absolute order of poetry is dependent upon *symbolique* because this alone reflects man's thirst for divine perfection and represents the sublime alternative in his spiritual duality. The poet, more than other men, is endowed with the comprehension of those supernatural correspondences. In regard to the artist's special perception, a comparison may be made between this sonnet and certain lines from the *Consolations* ("A mon ami Leroux," XVII) of Sainte-Beuve:

> Ils comprennent les flots, entendent les étoiles,
> Savent les noms des fleurs, et pour eux l'univers
> N'est qu'une seule idée en symboles divers.

The true destination of art and the route leading to it are serious preoccupations of the poet in "Les phares." The endless search for the Ideal which is undertaken on earth by the elect soul is represented by "cet ardent sanglot qui roule d'âge en âge/ Et vient mourir au bord de votre éternité!" The successful projection of the *extase de la vie* into the transcendental is completed only in passing the frontier of death into eternity. Like the way of the Cross, the way of the artist's quest is long and hard; unlike the agony of Jesus it is well lighted by the example of many precursors. The "ardent sanglot" is common to them all, and it would be fallacious to interpret the last stanza of the poem as a sign of revolt against God in order to establish the real nature of man's dignity. The whole tone of Baudelaire's poetry suggests that this dignity lies rather in the constant yearning of the exiled soul for reintegration in the divine perfection. This celebration in "Les phares" of the elite race of artists may be compared with that offered by Sainte-Beuve in his *Consolations* ("A mon ami Leroux," XVII):

> Le Seigneur qui, jaloux de l'œuvre de ses mains,
>
> .   .   .   .
>
> A des temps inégaux suscite par endroits
> Quelques rares mortels, grands, plus grands que les rois,
> Avec un sceau brillant sur leurs têtes sublimes,
>
> .   .   .   .

Tandis que sur ces fronts, hauts comme des sommets,
Le mystique Soleil ne se couche jamais.

A particularly tragic element in the poet's struggle against the *horreur* is the need to prostitute his genius for the amusement of the vulgar, merely in order to provide for a basic existence. The artistic hypocrisy enforced by material need is the painful theme of "La muse vénale":

Il te faut, pour gagner ton pain de chaque soir,
Comme un enfant de chœur, jouer de l'encensoir,
Chanter des *Te Deum* auxquels tu ne crois guère,
Ou, saltimbanque à jeun, étaler tes appas
Et ton rire trempé de pleurs qu'on ne voit pas,
Pour faire épanouir la rate du vulgaire.

For Baudelaire man's love for woman, in the flesh and in the spirit, participates in both the horror and the ecstasy of earthly life. One of the artificial paradises which seem to promise happiness to the poet in his early manhood is the sensual *volupté* offered in the carnal attractions of women. In Baudelaire's poetry, this appetite for the flesh after a brief triumph is either dissolved into a purely artistic contemplation of synesthetic values or becomes an exacerbating element in the total torment of ennui. As an example of the first of these two developments, that of a translation into plasticity, Chérix extracts the poem "Les bijoux" from the cycle of Jeanne Duval, reassigning it to the cycle of art.[29] The fifth and sixth strophes of the poem establish the poet's intention to emphasize his non-participation in the "trouble érotique" normally excited by the seduction of the flesh:

Et son bras et sa jambe, et sa cuisse et ses reins,
Polis comme de l'huile, onduleux comme un cygne,
Passaient devant mes yeux clairvoyants et sereins;
Et son ventre et ses seins, ces grappes de ma vigne,

29. Chérix, pp. 92-93.

S'avançaient, plus câlins que les Anges du mal,
Pour troubler le repos où mon âme était mise,
Et pour la déranger du rocher de cristal
Où, calme et solitaire, elle s'était assise.

The plastic embellishment of feminine nudity in this poem
reflects Baudelaire's own preference for the artificial in beauty,
a predilection expounded in his study on Constantin Guys, in
which the cosmetic art is eulogized.[30] The lover's carnal appetite seems to be neutralized in "Les bijoux" by his aesthetic
entrancement before an artistic spectacle. To infringe upon
the calm isolation of his "rocher de cristal" the mistress must
resort to more pointedly enticing erotic gestures. Her entice-
ment notwithstanding, the composition closes on a decidedly
plastic note.

The purely olfactory ingredient in the charm of women is
translated in "Parfum exotique" into an exotic sensuousness
rather than an erotic sensuality. By closing his eyes to the visual
reality of the mulatto woman, the poet creates from the scent
of her person a sensuous atmosphere by which he is able to
visualize the color and form of an exotic landscape:

Quand, les deux yeux fermés, en un soir chaud d'automne,
Je respire l'odeur de ton sein chaleureux,
Je vois se dérouler des rivages heureux
Qu'éblouissent les feux d'un soleil monotone;

The expressedly physical passion of the poem "Je t'adore à
l'égal de la voûte nocturne" is implicitly rejected, inasmuch as
the poet realizes the paradox of his spiritual situation. In his
lucidity he discerns that his profane love for Jeanne Duval is
the negation of sublime love:

Et t'aime d'autant plus, belle, que tu me fuis,
Et que tu me parais, ornement de mes nuits,

30. Baudelaire, "Guys, le peintre de la vie moderne," Œuvres complètes,
II, 619-622.

Plus ironiquement accumuler les lieues
Qui séparent mes bras des immensités bleues.

By her cruel frigidity, the mistress ironically confirms the futility of her lover's desire. The assault of this desire is ultimately
represented as tantamount to spiritual death in both participants: "Je m'avance à l'attaque, et je grimpe aux assauts, /
Comme après un cadavre un chœur de vermisseaux, . . ."

This irony inherent in purely erotic experience is reinforced
in "Tu mettrais l'univers entier dans ta ruelle" by the idea
that physical beauty, when used to satanic purposes, is inevitably diminished in relation to divine beauty, from which
it derives its law. This work, by the testimony of Prarond, is
one of the earliest poems recited by Baudelaire and refers to
Sara la Juive, who preceded Jeanne Duval in the poet's erotic
attentions. However, it could equally well apply to many
aspects of the "Vénus noire" herself. In this poem, physical
beauty diabolically dedicated to the passions of the flesh is
shown to be incapable, on its own vulgar level, of producing
anything for the poet but pain. Yet, in the ultimate paradox
of the divine order in life, this very betrayal by corrupted
beauty is transformed into a source of artistic creation for the
poet. In this sense the mistress is represented as a "salutaire
instrument."

Carnal love thus assumes for Baudelaire a double function:
it participates in the *horreur de la vie* and provides a temporary
escape from ennui. Thus, in a negative sense, it may be said
to participate also in the *extase* of man's worldly existence.
For these reasons, the cycle of Jeanne Duval in the *Fleurs du
Mal* is related both to the flesh and the spirit. The first of a
group of poems belonging to this cycle, "Sed non satiata,"
symbolizes basically the wavering of the poet's soul between
the temptations of the flesh and spiritual purity. In the final
tercet, the lover cannot accept for himself that part of Proser-

pine's destiny which demands her rule over Hades as Pluto's bride. In the remorse which follows the excesses of carnal passion, the poet is undoubtedly mindful of the original innocence of Demeter's daughter. The second poem of the group, "Le serpent qui danse," joins in many respects with "Les bijoux" in emphasizing the sterility and in neutralizing the sensual attraction of feminine beauty. By virtue of its last two stanzas, however, this composition is properly situated in the cycle of the flesh:

> Comme un flot grossi par la fonte
> Des glaciers grondants,
> Quand ta salive exquise monte
> Au bord de tes dents
>
> Je crois boire un vin de Bohême,
> Amer et vainqueur,
> Un ciel liquide qui parsème
> D'étoiles mon cœur!

As suggested by the title, a third poem, "Le Léthé," describes an attempt to seek in physical love total oblivion from the accumulating *horreur de la vie*. The essential tragedy of this poem is the lover's consciousness, in the very depth of carnal indulgence, that his soul is thereby destroyed in a predestined martyrdom to the tyranny of a heartless animal:

> A mon destin, désormais mon délice,
> J'obéirai comme un prédestiné;
> Martyr docile, innocent condamné,
> Dont la ferveur attise le supplice,
>
> Je sucerai, pour noyer ma rancœur,
> Le népenthès et la bonne ciguë
> Aux bouts charmants de cette gorge aiguë
> Qui n'a jamais emprisonné de cœur.

The remaining two poems of the group have a more spiritual tone. Jeanne Duval, although normally representing profane love, figures in the sonnet "Une nuit que j'étais près d'une affreuse Juive" as an antithesis of solely carnal passion. By the idealization of his desire for the absent dark Venus, Baudelaire devotes to her an almost Platonic cult:

> Je me pris à songer près de ce corps vendu
> A la triste beauté dont mon désir se prive.
>
> Je me représentai sa majesté native,
> Son regard de vigueur et de grâces armé,
> Ses cheveux qui lui font un casque parfumé,
> Et dont le souvenir pour l'amour me ravive.

Platonic admiration may well have characterized the earliest relationship between the poet and the mulatto. However, as the tercets suggest, that situation was not of the lover's choosing, for it resulted rather from frigid indifference than from inherent nobility in Jeanne's character. At least "Le balcon" leaves a calm and warm impression of the poet's feeling for her:

> Mère des souvenirs, maîtresse des maîtresses,
> —O toi, tous mes plaisirs, ô toi, tous mes devoirs!—
> Tu te rappelleras la beauté des caresses,
> La douceur du foyer et le charme des soirs,
> Mère des souvenirs, maîtresse des maîtresses!
>
> Les soirs illuminés par l'ardeur du charbon,
> Et les soirs au balcon, voilés de vapeurs roses;
> Que ton sein m'était doux! que ton cœur m'était bon!
> Nous avons dit souvent d'impérissables choses
> Les soirs illuminés par l'ardeur du charbon.

The tone of this poem accords with the generous appreciation of Jeanne contained in Baudelaire's letter to his mother of September 11, 1856,[31] written after his first serious rupture

31. Baudelaire, *Correspondance*, I, 396-400.

with his "Vénus noire." It is the last note sounded in the poems inspired by her which suggests anything other than acute pain and profound pessimism.

The spiritual aspect of Baudelairean love reaches its maximum intensity in the cycle of Madame Sabatier, where the poet testifies to a sublime inspiration tantamount to the true *extase de la vie.* The first of two poems in this cycle, "Que diras-tu ce soir, pauvre âme solitaire," establishes the angelic character of the "Vénus blanche" and affirms her influence over the poet for the comprehension of absolute beauty in art and in love:

—Nous mettrons notre orgueil à chanter ses louanges:
Rien ne vaut la douceur de son autorité;
Sa chair spirituelle a le parfum des Anges,
Et son œil nous revêt d'un habit de clarté.

Que ce soit dans la nuit et dans la solitude,
Que ce soit dans la rue et dans la multitude,
Son fantôme dans l'air danse comme un flambeau.

In the second poem of this cycle, the condemned "A celle qui est trop gaie," the spiritual element in Baudelaire's psychological duality enters into conflict with the excessive gaiety of Apollonie's feminine naturalness. The affronted gravity of the lover is moved to avenge itself upon the frivolity of a guardian angel who remains unconcerned with the metaphysical dilemma of man in general and with his dilemma in particular:

Ainsi, je voudrais, une nuit,
Quand l'heure des voluptés sonne,
Vers les trésors de ta personne
Comme un lâche ramper sans bruit,

Pour châtier ta chair joyeuse,
Pour meurtrir ton sein pardonné,

Et faire à ton flanc étonné
Une blessure large et creuse,

Et, vertigineuse douceur!
A travers ces lèvres nouvelles,
Plus éclatantes et plus belles,
T'infuser mon venin, ma sœur!

The aesthetic unity of the *Fleurs du Mal* renders convincing the view that a purely religious meaning lies beneath the apparently obscene sadism of the final stanza.[32] The venom infused by the lover symbolizes the consciousness of evil which should be active even in the midst of natural gaiety.

The psychological climate of the cycle of Marie Daubrun is governed by the appearance of an autumnal mood. Baudelaire seems conscious now of being on the reverse slope of his amatory career. Thus, this group of poems emphasizes the basic incommunicability of human souls blocked by some emotional catastrophe from the past. In its Indian summer, love can be no more than a consolation for pains suffered and goals unattained. The autumnal blending of light and gloom is reflected in "Ciel brouillé," a poem which achieves a delicate fusion of landscape with the image of the beloved. Rationally, the poet seeks consolation in the tender affection of the "Vénus verte," but the enigmatic sadness of her glance, like an autumn sky, arouses in him a nervous disquiet:

Tu rappelles ces jours blancs, tièdes et voilés,
Qui font se fondre en pleurs les cœurs ensorcelés,
Quand, agités d'un mal inconnu qui les tord,
Les nerfs trop éveillés raillent l'esprit qui dort.

The source of agitation is revealed in the last stanza of the poem, where, in a remarkable psychological catachresis, the decline of the beloved is foreshadowed:

32. Hubert, p. 238.

O femme dangereuse! ô séduisants climats!
Adorerai-je aussi ta neige et vos frimas,
Et saurai-je tirer de l'implacable hiver
Des plaisirs plus aigus que la glace et le fer?

The final verse presumably symbolizes the lover's suffering at the hands of an often cold and cruel mistress.

The painful paradox of autumnal love is most richly expressed in "Causerie," which completes the cycle of Marie Daubrun. The poet's heart, in which the affective strength has been paralyzed by the cruelties of wanton passion, is summoned to a loftier and more tender emotion by the suggested perfume of the beloved:

—Ta main se glisse en vain sur mon sein qui se pâme;
Ce qu'elle cherche, amie, est un lieu saccagé
Par la griffe et la dent féroce de la femme.—
Ne cherchez plus mon cœur; des monstres l'ont mangé.

Mon cœur est un palais flétri par la cohue;
On s'y soûle, on s'y tue, on s'y prend aux cheveux.
—Un parfum nage autour de votre gorge nue!—

In the final tercet the poet yields to the attraction of a more sublime beauty, abandoning the shreds of his lacerated heart to a last experience of love.

The principal psychological phenomenon in the autumnal cycle of Marie Daubrun is clearly the poet's pessimistic awareness of the death of his spirit, with the resulting wreck of his affective machinery. This gathering gloom is the climate which introduces the cycle of spleen proper, in which three of the poems offer a penetrating study of the collapse in the inner life and the consequent dominion of spiritual anguish. The first of these, "J'ai plus de souvenirs que si j'avais mille ans," emphasizes the role of the past and its painful resuscitations. The evidence of the poet's failures in love, in art, and in the management of his daily life lies hidden in a variety of receptacles, but the most commodious repository of all is the author's own memory, which holds a multitude of faded joys and bitter regrets. In the second part, the poet develops a striking parallel, in which, like some monument buried in the desert, the victim of ennui becomes himself abandoned in the oblivion of his own historical age, forgotten by the contemporary world.

In the allegory "Je suis comme le roi d'un pays pluvieux" the impotence of pathological boredom is projected chronologically into the characterization of another cruel *héautontimorouménos*—presumably a French king of the Renaissance. All the diversions of his court fail to reanimate this "cadavre hébété/ Où coule au lieu du sang l'eau verte du Léthé." The background of "un pays pluvieux" suggests the theme of artistic sterility, and by an historical displacement the author is enabled to create a poem on the frustration of poetic creativity by splenetic tedium vitae.

The paroxysm of spleen is achieved in "Quand le ciel bas et lourd pèse comme un couvercle." Like a psychiatric case history, this poem records the stages of ultimate cerebral chaos. The accumulating *horreur de la vie* exerts a physical pressure upon the victim's brain, and the world becomes for him a vast dungeon. The suffocating soul seeks desperately to escape from the compression of the mind, in the hope of transcending terrestrial existence and achieving an experience of the sublime. In the explosion of dementia which relaxes the tension of the brain, the captive spirit is ejected from its prison, only to remain thereafter disembodied—"errant et sans patrie." The mind has become the battleground on which the hope of a superior life has been vanquished by ennui. In this now barren enclosure of the conscience, the true victor, an acute mental anguish, has implanted its satanic ensign. The victim mourns the death of hope and the exile of his own soul.

With considerable logic, the cycle of spleen proper is followed in the 1857 edition of the *Fleurs* by "Brumes et pluies." At this stage in his personal tragedy the poet, whose heart is filled with the "choses funèbres" of his inadequate life in the world, views sympathetically those seasons which are by lyric tradition antipathetic to emotional exaltation. The victim of ennui loves the mists, frost, and rain of these "endormeuses saisons," for they spread a pall of oblivion over his mental and spiritual torment and inspire a truer expression of the inverted emotion in his soul. As agents of oblivion, the "blafardes saisons" are surpassed only by a different but related "endormeuse"—the morbid soporific of promiscuous sexual indulgence.

A small group of poems in the 1857 edition of the *Fleurs* presents a new aspect of evil and its attendant suffering, that of exterior social evil, especially in the human relations within a metropolis like Paris. This series does in fact represent the embryonic form of the "Tableaux parisiens," which appear in the 1861 edition. In one poem of the group, "Le jeu," gambling is treated as a typical Parisian vice and as one of the artificial escapes from the tyranny of the *vie insuffisante*. A forceful impression is created of the gaming house and its clients, but the important matter of this work is the poet's own attitude to the gamblers' passion. He pities them but is seized with envy before the spectacle of the "funèbre gaieté," which heartily animates the morally unconscious crowd running "avec ferveur à l'abîme béant." In his moral lucidity, he is aware of the suffering and spiritual damnation to which gaming will lead, but he envies those who have chosen an unreserved participation in the game of life at whatever cost. This attitude in the poem is amplified by Baudelaire's observations elsewhere: "La vie n'a qu'un charme vrai: c'est le charme du *Jeu*. Mais s'il nous est indifférent de gagner et de perdre?"[33]

33. Baudelaire, "Fusées," *Œuvres complètes*, II, 710.

Among the embryonic "Tableaux parisiens" of the first edition, two poems are concerned with a more idealized Paris than is normally presented in this cycle. Their presence in the larger cycle of spleen serves the contrapuntal function of contrasting the light and the darkness in Baudelaire's life. This contrast gives the measure of his collapse into anguish. In the first of these two, "La servante au grand cœur dont vous étiez jalouse," the ghost of the beloved Mariette returns to chide and to lament the physical and moral decay which has destroyed the manhood of a once innocent child. Spiritually conscious in his remorse, the poet has no acceptable answer to the indictment of his wasted years:

> Lorsque la bûche siffle et chante, si le soir,
> Calme, dans le fauteuil elle venait s'asseoir,
> Si, par une nuit bleue et froide de Décembre,
> Je la trouvais tapie en un coin de ma chambre,
> Grave, et venant du fond de son lit éternel
> Couver l'enfant grandi de son œil maternel,
> Que pourrais-je répondre à cette âme pieuse
> Voyant tomber des pleurs de sa paupière creuse?

A sharper counterpoint is achieved by the nostalgic evocation of the poet's childhood home in the second of the two poems, "Je n'ai pas oublié, voisine de la ville." The appeal of this brief work is enhanced by the frugal simplicity of the décor, enriched only by the splendor of the sun, which, as always for Baudelaire, ennobles and invests with poetic potential the most unpretentious elements of human experience. It is significant that the modest existence reconstituted in the poem is the short period of Madame Baudelaire's widowhood. The adverse effect of his mother's remarriage was certainly an important factor in the early formation of Baudelaire's personal ennui. This circumstance explains the particular position of the work in the thematic design of the *Fleurs du Mal*.

The division of "Spleen et Idéal" in the 1857 edition is unified by the quality of frenzied hatred in three poems which immediately follow "Le tonneau de la haine"—a mood appropriate to terminate this depiction of spleen in action.[34] These poems are "Le revenant," "Le mort joyeux," and "Sépulture." If this group has any serious importance for the development of Baudelaire's dualism, it must surely be as the expression of his acute irritation due to the erotic obtuseness or deceptions of his mistresses. This brief sequence of poems includes a sadistic fantasy directed against Jeanne Duval, "Le revenant," and the ironic malediction of an actress, "Sépulture," which certainly could have been inspired by Marie Daubrun.

In contrast to these poems of frenzy, a group of three poems appears to serve as diversions and consolations of the poet. "Tristesse de la lune," "La musique," and "La pipe" set an atmosphere of pacifying reverie which formally terminates the division of "Spleen et Idéal." In "Tristesse de la lune" the poet is united in reverie with the moon—that capricious guardian of artists and dreamers—who can perhaps rescue him from the ravages of earthly horror. "La musique" elaborates the theme of escape by a comparison of the poet's spiritual life with a ship—"vaisseau qui souffre." In the quatrains of this sonnet, the medium of music enables the author to fix his vision on the dimly perceived Ideal, which is equivalent to the order of poetry. The poet's soul, in its sublime transport, is borne toward its objective on a sea of music. In the tercets, the tempestuous ocean, by its convulsions, produces the author's interior upheaval. Music at times lulls the tormented spirit into oblivion. At other times it inspires the moral lucidity which engenders despair:

> Je sens vibrer en moi toutes les passions
> D'un vaisseau qui souffre:

34. Ruff, L'esprit du mal, p. 306.

Le bon vent, la tempête et ses convulsions
          Sur le sombre gouffre
Me bercent, et parfois le calme,—grand miroir
          De mon désespoir!

Whether it enables the poet to regain the lost paradise of the Ideal or merely confirms the gravity of his moral collapse, music is seen to be working always at the sublime pole of his spiritual duality. The final sonnet of the cycle, "La pipe," features a balm which soothes the mental and spiritual fatigue of the author.

The division "Spleen et Idéal" is immediately followed by the cycle of the most virulent "Fleurs du Mal." In this chapter of evil the central subject is not the author, or man in general, but those men and especially those women who have deliberately chosen evil in the form of sensual pleasure. Thus, from Baudelaire's standpoint, this series of poems has a true objectivity external to the author.[35] Concerning the poet's complicity in these poems through his sympathy with the sinners involved, Ruff observes:

> Baudelaire n'est ni prédicateur ni moraliste et ne s'affuble pas de leur masque. Il est un pécheur, pénétré de son indignité, et il le proclame avec toute la puissance de son art et toute la sincérité de sa conscience déchirée. S'il ose dénoncer d'autres fautes que les siennes, c'est seulement après en avoir assumé d'avance sa propre part, et s'il les dénonce, il ne les condamne pas, il ne les juge pas, il leur donne, avec un terrible avertissement, toute sa compassion fraternelle.[36]

The same critic adds, in reference to the sixth and seventh stanzas of "Lesbos":

> La première de ces deux strophes introduit l'explication audacieuse et profonde qui sera reprise dans les deux "Femmes damnées": la poursuite du mal est une manifesta-

35. *Ibid.*, p. 307.
36. *Ibid.*, p. 308.

tion d'angélisme, de l'aspiration à l'infini: "Chercheuses d'infini" . . . "Et fuyez l'infini que vous portez en vous." Ce n'est donc pas de l'immoralisme qui s'exprime dans les propos plus ou moins blasphématoires sur le juste et l'injuste, l'enfer et le ciel, mais déjà la révolte contre un monde qui ne tient pas les promesses du "radieux sourire entrevu vaguement au bord des autres cieux." Quant à la seconde strophe citée, elle fait briller sur cet enfer l'espérance chrétienne du pardon et de la rédemption par la souffrance.[37]

In "Une martyre," the first of the four poems in the cycle of the true "Fleurs du Mal," several characteristic Baudelairean features can be noted: the presentation of a corpse in contrast to the erotic orgy suggested by the décor; the presence of evil angels at the scene; the ravage of ennui upon an exasperated soul; the depravity of "désirs errants et perdus"; the triumph of pure idealism. The tragic significance of the erotic sadism presented in this poem is that its own horror is generated in a special attempt to escape, through the most extreme forms of sensual pleasure, from the general oppression of horror in the world. The idealism in the conclusion of the poem suggests the principle of "la guérison au bout d'une lame," found in Baudelaire's prose poem "Mademoiselle Bistouri."[38]

An analysis of the sin of carnal pleasure in its most extreme form is provided in "Delphine et Hippolyte." The dialogue between seduced and seductress in a Lesbian adventure marks seven stages in the waxing and waning of the ultimately tragic passion. The poem is terminated by a moral judgment delivered by the traditional chorus of Greek tragedy. In the first twelve lines of the poem, Hippolyte, having yielded to Delphine's exploratory caresses, is vaguely troubled by the thought of her fading innocence. The seductress, meanwhile, savors her approaching triumph, seeking in her victim's eyes a sign of acquiescent pleasure. In verses 25-34, which form the third

37. *Ibid.*, pp. 308-309.
38. Chérix, pp. 395-396.

stage, Delphine inveighs against the rival cult, warning Hippolyte of the destructive brutality natural to masculine sexuality. Delphine's diatribe is followed in the fourth stage by the gentle promise of an infinite ecstasy. The victim's reaction to this promise in the fifth stage is a mixture of fascination and disquiet. This element of anxiety is countered by Delphine in a disdainful rejection of morality as part of erotic passion. The basis of this disdain is expounded in verses 65-68:

> Celui qui veut unir dans un accord mystique
> L'ombre avec la chaleur, la nuit avec le jour,
> Ne chauffera jamais son corps paralytique
> A ce rouge soleil que l'on nomme l'amour!

In the last stage of the dialogue, Hippolyte reveals that her soul has become engulfed in emotional chaos, in which her appetite for the supreme *volupté* is only multiplied by satisfaction. The only possible respite from this anguish is the annihilation of the spirit in the morbid lassitude which follows consummation of the Sapphic passion. The moral perspicacity of the chorus in verses 85-104 illuminates the paradox in the career of the protagonists. The inverted cult of these *chercheuses d'infini* is ironic precisely because they reject the "honnêteté" which derives from man's spiritual aspiration toward divine purity. Thus, they refuse the sublime ecstasy itself for which they thirst, condemning themselves to a permanent separation from God. Hubert observes that, even if the chorus is not considered, the moral alternative in this poem is clear, since the author subtly reveals the suffering born of perversity.[39]

The flavor of Greek tragedy is also apparent in the poem "Femmes damnées." Five tableaux presenting different aspects of Lesbianism lead to a chorus-like climax, in which the poet identifies his own emotions with the appetites and remorse of

39. Hubert, p. 260.

the devotees. The first stanza conveys an impression merely of vague yearning, against the stylized landscape of a painter's Lesbos. The second tableau suggests the timorous beginnings of inversion in a sisterhood of childish innocence. The third stanza introduces violent temptations such as might have confronted Saint Anthony amid "les rochers pleins d'apparitions." In the fourth tableau the fever of profane desire is heightened by a Bacchanalian orgy. Finally, in the fifth stanza, the sadistic pleasures of flagellation and the scapulary plunge the perverted sisterhood into new depths of depravity. The chorus explains the essential tragedy of the cult in terms of a permanently frustrated metaphysical aspiration. It is man's nature to be drawn in part to the supernatural, and in this aspect of his character he becomes the "grand esprit contempteur de la réalité." It is a matter of human experience that his search for the infinite exaltation frequently leads him into abnormal and depraved practices.

The poet delivers an ironic criticism of his own acedia in "La Béatrice." Borrowing the point of view of Satan, he develops in the first two stanzas of the poem a highly cynical retort to his own *clamor de profundis*. The temptations and persecutions which have contributed to the personal disaster of Baudelaire's *vie insuffisante* are symbolized by a cloud of vicious demons who gloat with cruel curiosity upon his agony. These morally insensitive devils are incapable of comprehending the soul-rending dualism within the poet's conscience, which has culminated in an inertia of the will comparable to the indecision of Hamlet. In the last stanza the victim's self-respect is shown to be capable of transcending the vindictive mockery of the spirits, were it not for the spiritual perfidy of the idolized mistress. This un-Dantesque Beatrice is the source of the most deadly venom, because her infidelity and secret derision have profaned a love which bore for the naïve lover the promise of the sublime. Since she is adequately defined by her perfidious function, the precise identity of the traitress is of small import, though we can without strain recognize in her some traits of Jeanne, Apollonie, and Marie.

The gravest order of evil—the sin of revolt against God, not now by the flesh, but by the mind and in the spirit—is represented in the formal cycle of "Révolte." It has already been noted, in regard to "Le reniement de saint Pierre," one of the *Douze poèmes* of 1852, that Baudelaire held this ultimate category of sin to be the result of typical human sophistry. In two poems of the cycle, "Abel et Caïn" and "Les litanies de Satan," the apparent revolt against God, which does not represent the personal attitude of the author, partakes both of the *horreur* and the *extase* of life. As a divergence from God the spiritual revolt is certainly to be equated with sin. Yet the very rebellion emanates from a lack of confidence in the divine benevolence, from despair that the lofty projects of the highest human idealism can ever be fulfilled. Such idealistic conceptions, when related to the supernatural, certainly participate in the *extase* of human existence. The profane and the sublime are thus intermingled in the spiritual tragedy of revolt summarized in this earlier declaration from "Le reniement de saint Pierre":

> Certes, je sortirai, quant à moi, satisfait
> D'un monde où l'action n'est pas la sœur du rêve;
> Puissé-je user du glaive et périr par le glaive!

Social and economic inequality are the sources of rebellion in "Abel et Caïn," where a clear contrast is drawn between material ease and privation, between social acceptance and rejection. In a reversal of the values proclaimed in the Beatitudes, God is portrayed in this poem as smiling complacently on an affluent nineteenth-century society presumably enjoying the fruits of commercial expansion and the industrial revolution. The angelic host appears gratified by the comfortable worship of a hypocritical middle-class religiosity. In the robust health of its own well-being the affluent race multiplies, but the expansive aspirations are stifled by the constraining reality of the misery of the poor. The uprising incited in the second part of the composition certainly suggests the revolutionary spirit of the 1840's, but, more than a political revolution, it is the desperate gesture of modern humanitarianism before the cold inscrutability of God's purpose in history. The majesty of the incarnate God is actually confirmed by the overthrow of an idol that symbolizes only a social establishment of religiosity. Though Baudelaire is here dealing with revolt against a false Christianity, it is doubtful whether he saw in the vengeful spirit of revolutionary socialism anything more than another idolatrous sophistry.

The supplication to the Devil in "Les litanies de Satan" should be considered rather as an affirmation of affinity between Satan and the poet than as a true gesture of revolt against God. The interpretation of the poem in this sense becomes inevitable when it is read in conjunction with those stanzas of "Bénédiction" which treat the destiny of the poet as a Heaven-sent missionary. By divine decree, the poet is an expatriate in man's world, temporarily separated from the heavenly paradise by his artistic mission, but under the permanent guardianship of the angels. Because, by virtue of poetic intuition, he is the interpreter of the transcendental *symbolique,* and because his highest conception of beauty is allied to a sense of tragic heroism, the poet finds a parallel between his situation and that of the banished Lucifer, called "le plus savant et le plus beau des Anges." In accordance with the aesthetic principle of the *Fleurs du Mal,* Baudelaire has sought his poetic substance in sin, vice, and suffering—the improbable treasures hidden in Hell. But, in so doing, he has proposed, as an acceptable offering to God and for the purification of his own spirit, a moral alternative to the rebellious protest against the horror of the *vie insuffisante*. Milton's Satan, on the contrary, following the advice of his lieutenant Belial, plans to use the riches of his Hell for the insidious destruction of man. The concluding prayer in the "Litanies" contains a rebellious sophistry which is a potential danger not so much for Baudelaire as for the other clairvoyant modern poets—Nerval, Rimbaud, Mallarmé, and their successors—to whom he is related. The spreading branches of the Tree of Knowledge, with their occult and cabalistic fruits, offer a challenge to the divine control of knowledge. The *voyant* may seek, in the perfection of his own poetic intuition, to rival the unique creative power of God.

Ruff remarks that in the 1857 edition of the *Fleurs* the last two divisions, "Le vin" and "La mort," represent solutions to the desperate predicaments of evil suggested by the chapters entitled "Fleurs du Mal" and "Révolte." In his view "Le vin" is only a half-serious chapter, of purely relative and temporary effectiveness, whereas "La mort" presents a definite resolution of the problem of evil in the earthly existence.[40] In "Le vin du solitaire" the poet seeks escape from his own crushing ennui in the chance experiences of nocturnal wanderings in the Parisian suburbs. The scenes of human misery which confront him serve only to intensify his spiritual suffering while plunging him into an acute feeling of isolation. For his worn-out spirit, wine in turn serves as an artificial evasion, restoring to him illusions of a triumphant life. In "Le vin des amants" wine, normally only a temporary consolation, is presented as a means of transcending the insufficiency of life in the world. This inadequacy presumably includes the inevitable wounds and disenchantments of erotic love. Within their very passion, the lovers are drawn by a feverish yearning for the elusive infinite happiness. The intoxication offered by wine operates as a winged phoenix which bears the couple in a whirlwind

40. Ruff, *L'esprit du mal*, p. 316.

ascent to a visionary paradise. But even in the delirium of their shared exaltation they preserve a calm sense of direction toward a "ciel féerique et divin"—another indication of Baudelaire's poetic preoccupation with the *extase de la vie*.

*   *   *

The findings of the preceding survey conducted on the earliest edition of the *Fleurs du Mal* give evidence of the aesthetic unity which is so remarkable a quality in Baudelaire's amplified and rearranged masterpiece of 1861. Even in this first edition, the a posteriori arrangement of chapters shows a clear awareness of the dominating spirit of evil suggested by the title. Marcel Ruff, nevertheless, argues authoritatively that Baudelaire was not governed by the demands of any aesthetic cadre until the significant years between the first and second editions.[41] During this period, the crystallization of his thought under the pressure of his personal life produced an aggravated awareness of personal responsibility in sin and of the satanic inspiration of evil in human life. Such a movement in his thought gradually brought about a conscious design in which to incorporate the thirty-five new poems of the 1861 edition. Within this number, those poems which were interpolated in the division of "Spleen et Idéal" accomplish an intensification of despair in comparison with the 1857 version. The essential invalidity of all evasions of the *horreur* is more conclusively demonstrated, and erotic passion in particular assumes the nature of an uncompromising cruelty. The purely psychological tone of "Spleen et Idéal" in 1857 yields in 1861 to a theological emphasis, in which is posed the urgent choice between spiritual salvation or damnation. This exigent alternative, together with the deepening of despair, will be examined in the subsequent chapter dealing with Baudelaire's increased spiritu-

41. *Ibid.*, pp. 318-330.

ality. The rest of the new poems appearing in the 1861 edition belong to the new cycle, "Tableaux parisiens," in which the presence of evil is examined from a less personal, more generally human point of view. Since this division is more relevant to the matter of modernism in the poetry of Sainte-Beuve and Baudelaire, it will be considered later in a specific investigation of that quality.

Sainte-Beuve's *Poésies de Joseph Delorme* and the *Fleurs du Mal*, even in the 1857 edition, both express the fundamental theme of Romantic lyricism—the only theme which survives the evaporation of stylized rhetoric and personal sentiment. It is that of the moral and psychological bipolarity existing in the human consciousness. This bipolarity is created by the fragmentation of absolute unity; and this fragmentation is inherent in the phenomena of the *horreur de la vie*. The reintegration of the fractured absolute wholeness becomes the ultimate aspiration of every spiritual human being. Both the means to this end and the end itself participate in the *extase de la vie*. Blin has described this aspiration to reintegration as "la jalousie de la vie suffisante."[42]

Baudelaire, in the 1857 edition of the *Fleurs*, effectively typifies through his personal experience the anguish of his generation. Yet in his case there are two different approaches to the question of *la vie suffisante*. From the psychological point of view, absolute unity is seen in terms of a lost paradise of primitive childhood felicity. To this paradisiac wholeness the barrier is, in Baudelaire's scheme, the earthly *horreur*. The final evidence of this fragmentation is the existence on earth of differentiated human personalities. The first antidote to the *horreur de la vie* is therefore conceived, in Baudelaire's own terms, as "la vaporisation du Moi." Psychologically, this dissolution of the poet's ego is attempted through temporary *extases*—evasive intoxicants which suggest the paradise of the

42. Blin, p. 128.

absolute whole, where "tout n'est qu'ordre et beauté,/ Luxe, calme et volupté." Among these we may include the artistic eroticism inspired by Jeanne Duval and the autumnal and less frenzied affection devoted to Marie Daubrun. Such experiences—together with the more conventional evasions procured by hashish, opium, and wine—are intended to reintegrate the fragmentation of the infinite absolute. False *extases* such as these inevitably result in the tragic irony of remorse. Yet the most important of all temporary evasions of life's horror is the poetic transformation of immediate reality into the permanent reality of the infinite whole. Poetic creation is seen to possess two natures: the nature of a true but temporary *extase*; and, inasmuch as poetry manifests absolute truth, the nature of the infinite unity. Paradoxically, poetic creation utilizes the very fragmentation implicit in the mystic principle of correspondences and in the concept of the universal analogy to arrive at ultimate reintegration. Through poetry the horror of earthly reality is transformed by the temporary *extase* into the infinite ecstasy of the transcendental whole. By the principle of universal analogy, artistic creation participates in the *vie suffisante*.

The other approach to the *vie suffisante* is theological, and from this point of view the integrated absolute whole is God. The poet's soul is thus an elect soul, for whom the fragmentation in earthly finitude is both a mission and a sacrifice. The mission is to communicate the truth of the Creator by the poetic manipulation of his creation. The sacrifice is that of the poet's integral infinitude to the vulgarity of human finitude. The manifold *horreur de la vie* is seen theologically as Jansenist sin, with its root in original sin. The hope of reintegration for the sacrificed poet is sought in the spiritual love of an Apollonie Sabatier, in vicarious intercession through reversibility, and in a life of repentant piety.

The sense of deprivation which received its varied expression

6. *A theological urgency—the* Fleurs du Mal *of 1861*

After the first edition of the *Fleurs du Mal*, Sainte-Beuve remarked in a letter to Baudelaire (July 20, 1857) that the younger poet had chosen the limited territory of the infernal. Referring to the spiritual transformation—"l'aube blanche et vermeille"—described in "L'aube spirituelle," he advocated for his young follower the cultivation in future verse of the "ange" who is awakened in "la brute assoupie." He went on to suggest that the *Fleurs* of 1857 should have included more poems devoted to the sublime alternative, in which these curious dreams of evil might dissolve under the light of divine grace. Sainte-Beuve emphasized his own *Consolations* as an example of the dispersal by divine inspiration of the complex "Tentation de saint Antoine" represented by the Delorme poems. Notwithstanding the keen moral perception of Baudelaire's first edition, it must be admitted that the poems do not create the impression of an insistent metaphysical anxiety or of a spiritual biography in specifically Christian terms. The author accomplishes merely a dense survey of man's psychic complexity, through which penetrates a basic pattern of moral duality.

During the period between 1857 and 1861, however, the gathering despair of the poet's personal life added a much greater urgency to his metaphysical anxiety and to the question of life beyond the grave. Many cycles of that personal life had been painfully closed. Thus, the second edition of the *Fleurs* includes a number of additional poems which give a note of finality to the author's several failures. By conveying the utter sterility of the profane pole in man's duality, these compositions suggest the sublime alternative. In this sense, though neither Christ nor even a unified God is evoked, the *Fleurs* added in the 1861 edition perform for Baudelaire the function of the *Consolations* in the aesthetic pattern of Sainte-Beuve's poetic creation. But for the younger poet the sublime alternative never found the obvious poetic development that his mentor had counseled. In keeping with his personal diffidence, Baudelaire used his poetic process to imply rather than to specify the nature of the transcending Divinity and of Christian redemption.

In the 1857 edition of the *Fleurs du Mal,* the poem "Bénédiction," in which the mission and sacrifice of the poet are given elaborate treatment, was followed immediately by "Le soleil," in which the principal theme is the poet's search for artistic inspiration in the everyday life of Paris. The gravity and closer aesthetic unity of the 1861 edition created a need for a concise but vivid emblem to signify the complexity of the poet's personal drama as an artist exiled in the world. This need was satisfied by "L'albatros," which took final form in 1859 and assumed the position formerly held by "Le soleil." The multivalence of the poet's role in the mortal life is presented in the final stanza of the poem:

Le Poète est semblable au prince des nuées
Qui hante la tempête et se rit de l'archer;
Exilé sur le sol au milieu des huées,
Ses ailes de géant l'empêchent de marcher.

Baudelaire's friend Asselineau requested the addition of a
stanza to emphasize the awkwardness and uneasiness of the
symbolic bird in its terrestrial exile.[1] This request was met by
the addition of what is now the third stanza:

Ce voyageur ailé, comme il est gauche et veule!
Lui, naguère si beau, qu'il est comique et laid!
L'un agace son bec avec un brûle-gueule,
L'autre mime, en boitant, l'infirme qui volait!

The various cycles of eroticism in the 1857 edition describe
the poet's attempts to escape from the *horreur de la vie* in the
seductive embrace of robust feminine beauty. By 1861, however, Baudelaire was sufficiently convinced of the false nature
of this ecstasy to want to give specific expression to the deception. Hence, in the second edition of the *Fleurs*, a poem entitled "Le masque" unmasks the lie inherent in the promise of
happiness by carnal passion. The "souris fin et voluptueux"
and the "long regard sournois, langoureux et moqueur" of the
admirer's first impression are revealed in the light of truth to
be but "une exquise grimace." The erotic diversions pursued
by voluptuous woman merely conceal a suffering which is
described in the poem as emanating from the inevitability of
living:

—Elle pleure, insensé, parce qu'elle a vécu!
Et parce qu'elle vit! Mais ce qu'elle déplore
Surtout, ce qui la fait frémir jusqu'aux genoux,
C'est que demain, hélas! il faudra vivre encore!
Demain, après-demain, et toujours!—comme nous!

1. Eugène Crépet, *Ch. Baudelaire* (Paris: Albert Massein, 1928), p. 311.

The psychological truth is that life demands engagement for every man in the metaphysical anguish of his own spiritual duality. The lassitude of human existence derives from the constant frustration of man's idealism under the conditions of the world in which he is condemned to live.

In the cycle of *Fleurs* devoted to the nature of beauty, two poems in the 1857 edition set forth somewhat contradictory aesthetic values. "La Beauté" emphasized the characteristics of impassivity and inscrutability, whereas "L'Idéal" expressed the poet's preference for heroines of full-blooded passion—passion being understood in the sense of unrestrained engagement in the drama of spiritual bipolarity. The addition to the 1861 edition, "L'hymne à la Beauté," is more in harmony with "L'Idéal." In the later poem, beauty, which is incidentally the source of poetic inspiration, is attracted to both poles of man's moral duality:

> Viens-tu du ciel profond ou sors-tu de l'abîme,
> O Beauté? ton regard, infernal et divin,
> Verse confusément le bienfait et le crime,
> Et l'on peut pour cela te comparer au vin.

Inasmuch as beauty maintains an equilibrium between these two poles, it reflects the harmony implicit in the title and in the aesthetic unity of the *Fleurs du Mal*. "Horreur" and "Meurtre" are not the least of its adornments at the profane pole of its dual nature, but at the sublime pole it can lead the poet to the rediscovery of his lost paradise, since it transforms the spiritual ugliness of the world and relieves the oppressive weight of ennui. The fact that the beauty envisaged in this poem lives in the full passion of man's spiritual anguish provides an appropriate link between the division of the *Fleurs* devoted to abstract considerations of art and the personal cycles of the love poems which present the erotic evasion of the *horreur de la vie* in all its complexity.

In the 1857 edition, the sonnet "Parfum exotique" realized one of the important functions of the cycle associated with Jeanne Duval—the evocation through memory of Baudelaire's exotic world. An addition of 1861, "La chevelure," is an elaboration of the earlier poem, which it immediately follows. Here the vaguer synesthesia of the sonnet is given both precision and intensity by the fusion of two images. The concrete object of the present moment, "la chevelure," is identified with the medium of memory, "l'océan":

> Tu contiens, mer d'ébène, un éblouissant rêve
> De voiles, de rameurs, de flammes et de mâts:
> Un port retentissant où mon âme peut boire
> A grands flots le parfum, le son et la couleur;
> Où les vaisseaux, glissant dans l'or et dans la moire,
> Ouvrent leurs vastes bras pour embrasser la gloire
> D'un ciel pur où frémit l'éternelle chaleur.

In the last stanza the exotic element is made to crystallize in the concrete "chevelure," which thus becomes a permanent source of poetic memory. The order of poetry finally triumphs over the immediate eroticism inspired by the "Vénus noire" —which fact helps to explain her long and powerful domination of the poet.

Three poems were added to the cycle of Jeanne Duval in the 1861 edition to symbolize the essentially satanic nature of carnal love. The first of these, "Chanson d'après-midi," is separated from the main body of the cycle but contains unmistakable references to the sensual enslavement of the poet. The infernal character of the idol who will deaden the pains of ennui by the evocation of a distant paradise is established in the first stanza of the poem. The enslaved heart is tormented by the enigmatic ambivalence in the soul of the tyrant, but there is no strong revolt against this profane tyranny, for the exotic seduction of the mistress apparently illumines the gloom in the poet's soul, like an "Explosion de chaleur/ Dans ma noire Sibérie!" The second poem, "Duellum," presents love in warlike terms as a duel of attrition between two hearts ripened by experience and ulcerated by mutual disillusion. The relatively healthy quarrels of love's first encounters yield in time to the corrosive poison of a hatred swollen to the stature of a passion:

> Deux guerriers ont couru l'un sur l'autre; leurs armes
> Ont éclaboussé l'air de lueurs et de sang.
> Ces jeux, ces cliquetis du fer sont les vacarmes
> D'une jeunesse en proie à l'amour vagissant.
>
> Les glaives sont brisés! comme notre jeunesse,
> Ma chère! Mais les dents, les ongles acérés,
> Vengent bientôt l'épée et la dague traîtresse.
> —O fureur des cœurs mûrs par l'amour ulcérés!

The abyss of the lovers' hatred is equated finally to a theological Hell, no less infernal for being "de nos amis peuplé." The repudiation of eros tacitly implies the desirability of its sublime alternative—agape. In this sense, the poem faithfully performs its function as a *Fleur du Mal*.

The moral anxiety activated in the presence of profane passion is presented with greater subtlety in the last of the three poems, "Le possédé." The tragedy of the soul's enslavement to the senses is enacted in a simple antithesis of two symbols— "soleil" and "lune." As normally with Baudelaire, the sun represents poetic creation and the spirituality of the sublime pole where it is inspired. The moon is identified with the "Vénus noire." Brilliant only with reflected light, it duplicates the eclipse of the sun. In this eclipse, which symbolizes the spiritual death of the artist, poet and mistress are first engulfed in a common inferno of ennui. Subsequently, the reillumination of "la lune," with light borrowed from a satanic source, reanimates the woman in an environment of profane pleasure which dissolves the earlier ennui:

> . . . Pourtant, si tu veux aujourd'hui,
> Comme un astre éclipsé qui sort de la pénombre,
> Te pavaner aux lieux que la Folie encombre,
> C'est bien! Charmant poignard, jaillis de ton étui!

The lover's enslavement is revealed in the final tercet of the sonnet to be entirely sensual. Whether the "Vénus noire" be numbed in the "nuit noire" of morbid ennui or falsely enlivened in the "rouge aurore" of base passions, she is adored as "mon cher Belzébuth"—an instrument of satanic tyranny. Like "Duellum," this poem intends a real denial of the profane postulation of man's soul. Similarly, there is implied in this denial the secret disquiet of the universal appetite for the sublime Infinite.

Except for a dedicatory poem, the cycle of Jeanne Duval is closed in 1861 with the quartet of sonnets grouped as "Fantôme." In this series the poet faces the cruel truth of Jeanne's moral and physical decrepitude, evident from the end of 1858. The first sonnet, "Les ténèbres," describes the illumination of the poet's own gloom by the haunting memory of his mistress in her earlier grace and splendor. He reinforces his image in "Le parfum" by recalling the scents formerly exuded by the beloved's tresses and garments:

> De ses cheveux élastiques et lourds,
> Vivant sachet, encensoir de l'alcôve,
> Une senteur montait, sauvage et fauve,
>
> Et des habits, mousseline ou velours,
> Tout imprégnés de sa jeunesse pure,
> Se dégageait un parfum de fourrure.

In the third sonnet of the group, "Le cadre," the poet remembers that the natural nude beauty of his "Vénus noire" was always enhanced by the artificial luxury of her adornment or environment:

> Ainsi bijoux, meubles, métaux, dorure,
> S'adaptaient juste à sa rare beauté;
> Rien n'offusquait sa parfaite clarté,
> Et tout semblait lui servir de bordure.

The final sonnet, "Le portrait," contains both a cry of horror and an heroic defiance in the presence of physical decay. Sickness and death destroy the glory of beauty in its prime. Time destroys life and, in the fading portrait of the mulatto woman, art itself. But the final tercet affirms the security of the beloved image in the poet's memory:

> Noir assassin de la Vie et de l'Art,
> Tu ne tueras jamais dans ma mémoire
> Celle qui fut mon plaisir et ma gloire!

The general luminosity of "Fantôme" has a calming effect which is in marked contrast to the dramatic bitterness which characterizes the other 1861 additions to the containing cycle. Yet it must not be forgotten that the actual circumstances in which this series of sonnets was composed gave little promise of anything but acute despair in the relations between Baudelaire and Jeanne Duval.

As an escape from the bitter disillusion in which he is left at the conclusion of the Jeanne Duval cycle, Baudelaire cultivates a "mensonge," the nature of which is explored in the poem of 1861 entitled "Semper eadem." It provides a convincing historical and artistic link between the cycle of the "Vénus noire" and that of the "Vénus blanche"—Apollonie Sabatier. The latter, with characteristically petulant gaiety, seeks the cause of the poet's mysterious sadness. She learns that the solution to the enigma lies in a very common philosophical thesis:

—Quand notre cœur a fait une fois sa vendange,
Vivre est un mal. C'est un secret de tous connu,

Une douleur très-simple et non mystérieuse,
Et, comme votre joie, éclatante pour tous.

The whole painful course of the poet's love for Jeanne is represented by "sa vendange" and in the resulting despair, "Plus encor que la Vie,/ La Mort nous tient souvent par des liens subtils." Baudelaire's personal history reveals that what he sought in his relationship with Madame Sabatier was the spiritual intoxication of a Platonic love. The tranquil nature of the desired evasion is affirmed in the final tercet of the sonnet:

Laissez, laissez mon cœur s'enivrer d'un *mensonge*,
Plonger dans vos beaux yeux comme dans un beau songe,
Et sommeiller longtemps à l'ombre de vos cils!

The poet's lucidity, however, prevents his giving any permanency to this deceptive consolation. It remains a beautiful lie.

Among the 1861 additions to the cycle of Marie Daubrun, the "Chant d'automne" prolongs and intensifies the lucid pessimism of an 1857 poem, "Causerie." In this later composition the poet welcomes the consolation of autumnal love, while recognizing its essential brevity:

Et pourtant aimez-moi, tendre cœur! soyez mère,
Même pour un ingrat, même pour un méchant;
Amante ou sœur, soyez la douceur éphémère
D'un glorieux automne ou d'un soleil couchant.

The essential futility of love in the late season depends upon both the past and the future. The heart's only "vendange" of love—"le soleil rayonnant sur la mer"—has left it a "lieu saccagé/ Par la griffe et la dent féroce de la femme." The task of the consoling love will not be long, for somewhere a coffin is being hastily nailed. In the first part of the poem, all the signs of autumn are a fateful premonition of the tomb:

> Bientôt nous plongerons dans les froides ténèbres;
> Adieu, vive clarté de nos étés trop courts!
> J'entends déjà tomber avec des chocs funèbres
> Le bois retentissant sur le pavé des cours.
>
> Tout l'hiver va rentrer dans mon être: colère,
> Haine, frissons, horreur, labeur dur et forcé,
> Et, comme le soleil dans son enfer polaire,
> Mon cœur ne sera plus qu'un bloc rouge et glacé.
>
> J'écoute en frémissant chaque bûche qui tombe;
> L'échafaud qu'on bâtit n'a pas d'écho plus sourd.
> Mon esprit est pareil à la tour qui succombe
> Sous les coups du bélier infatigable et lourd.

The final melancholy truth is the failure of the present consolation to efface the radiance of love's earlier harvest or of an earlier dream of paradise:

> J'aime de vos longs yeux la lumière verdâtre,
> Douce beauté, mais tout aujourd'hui m'est amer,
> Et rien, ni votre amour, ni le boudoir, ni l'âtre,
> Ne me vaut le soleil rayonnant sur la mer.

Another addition to the cycle of the "Vénus verte" in the 1861 edition, "A une Madone," occupies the place held by "L'héautontimorouménos" in 1857. It also is concerned with the theme of the earlier poem—the conception of erotic passion as an exchange of suffering. In a confession of suspicion and jealousy addressed to the mistress who has left him for Théodore de Banville, the poet purposes to wound both the beloved and himself, since he has raised to her "Un autel souterrain au fond de ma détresse":

> Enfin, pour compléter ton rôle de Marie,
> Et pour mêler l'amour avec la barbarie,

Volupté noire! des sept Péchés capitaux,
Bourreau plein de remords, je ferai sept Couteaux
Bien affilés, et, comme un jongleur insensible,
Prenant le plus profond de ton amour pour cible,
Je les planterai tous dans ton Cœur pantelant,
Dans ton Cœur sanglotant, dans ton Cœur ruisselant!

The obvious religious parody contained in the poem serves the familiar Baudelairean function of emphasizing the separation of carnal passion from the sublime pole in man's nature.

In the opinion of Jacques Crépet,[2] the personal inspiration of the "Sonnet d'automne" is uncertain, but this edition of 1861 helps in any case to establish more clearly the nature of autumnal love and of the carnal passion which it is intended to console. The tercets of this sonnet express the desire for a tranquil love devoid of passion. The conditions which would preclude the fulfillment of this desire are also specified in a closely linked antithesis which reveals the armory of profane love:

Aimons-nous doucement. L'Amour dans sa guérite,
Ténébreux, embusqué, bande son arc fatal.
Je connais les engins de son vieil arsenal:

Crime, horreur et folie! . . . .

"Sisina," first appearing in the 1861 edition, presents the erotic element in images from the hunt and the Revolution. A dynamic Diana and a forceful popular heroine, Théroigne de Méricourt, symbolize the aggressive initiative of carnal passion:

Imaginez Diane en galant équipage,
Parcourant les forêts ou battant les halliers,
Cheveux et gorge au vent, s'enivrant de tapage,
Superbe et défiant les meilleurs cavaliers!

2. Baudelaire, *Fleurs*, pp. 408-409. See editor's note.

Avez-vous vu Théroigne, amante du carnage,
Excitant à l'assaut un peuple sans souliers,
La joue et l'œil en feu, jouant son personnage,
Et montant, sabre au poing, les royaux escaliers?

In the case of Madame Sisina Nieri, *demi-mondaine* friend of
Madame Sabatier, the heart "ravagé par la flamme" is capable
of compassion "devant les suppliants qui s'en montrent
dignes."

The sobering allegory "Une gravure fantastique" is inserted
in the 1861 edition of the *Fleurs* as a desirable link between
the stylized frenzy of "Sépulture" and the acute pessimism of
"Le tonneau de la haine." This composition presents the
apocalyptic figure of Death suggested by an engraving of the
eighteenth-century English artist, Mortimer:

Ce spectre singulier n'a pour toute toilette,
Grotesquement campé sur son front de squelette,
Qu'un diadème affreux sentant le carnaval.

. . . .

Le cavalier promène un sabre qui flamboie
Sur les foules sans nom que sa monture broie,
Et parcourt, comme un prince inspectant sa maison,
Le cimetière immense et froid, sans horizon,
Où gisent, aux lueurs d'un soleil blanc et terne,
Les peuples de l'histoire ancienne et moderne.

Toward the end of the division of "Spleen et Idéal" in the
1861 edition, four poems were added in which extreme ennui
tends to effect a transformation of all joy and pleasure into
grief and distaste. The ultimate stage in this transformation is
the nullification of exterior reality as an influence on the poet's
psyche. The first of these poems, "Obsession," presents an
attempt to achieve total abolition of the self by a denial of
objective reality in nature. The attempt is condemned to fail-

ure, however, because the interior psychic life of the individual cannot be separated from the forms of the created universe:

> Grands bois, vous m'effrayez comme des cathédrales;
> Vous hurlez comme l'orgue; et dans nos cœurs maudits,
> Chambres d'éternel deuil où vibrent de vieux râles,
> Répondent les échos de vos *De profundis.*
>
> Je te hais, Océan! tes bonds et tes tumultes,
> Mon esprit les retrouve en lui; ce rire amer
> De l'homme vaincu, plein de sanglots et d'insultes,
> Je l'entends dans le rire énorme de la mer.
>
> Comme tu me plairais, ô nuit! sans ces étoiles
> Dont la lumière parle un langage connu!
> Car je cherche le vide, et le noir, et le nu!

Even darkness itself—the most advanced form of nullified objectivity—is illumined by a thousand memories reanimated in the psyche by a creative imagination:

> Mais les ténèbres sont elles-mêmes des toiles
> Où vivent, jaillissant de mon œil par milliers,
> Des êtres disparus aux regards familiers.

The second poem, "Le goût du néant," envisages a complete disengagement from the motivations of mortal life:

> Résigne-toi, mon cœur, dors ton sommeil de brute.
> Esprit vaincu, fourbu! Pour toi, vieux maraudeur,
> L'amour n'a plus de goût, non plus que la dispute;

Even the sublime Ideal evoked through poetic creation appears to fade, for "Le Printemps adorable a perdu son odeur!" and the poet has bidden farewell to the "chants du cuivre et soupirs de la flûte!"

In the third poem, "Alchimie de la douleur," the poet is presented as accursed with the magical powers of Midas, "Le plus triste des alchimistes." By some satanic power, he reverses the values of natural reality:

> Par toi je change l'or en fer
> Et le paradis en enfer;
> Dans le suaire des nuages
>
> Je découvre un cadavre cher,
> Et sur les célestes rivages
> Je bâtis de grands sarcophages.

The clouds become an image of the poet's psychic life—a shroud enclosing the "cadavre cher" of the grievous memories summoned from the past by the alchemist. The logical parallel between "sarcophages" in the final tercet and "Sépulture" in the first quatrain suggests that the expected paradise of "les célestes rivages" has been transformed into an inferno by the erection of monuments to the painful experiences of the poet's earlier life.[3]

In the fourth poem, "Horreur sympathique," the sky again reflects the poet's inner hell, created by his cursed gift of alchemy:

> Cieux déchirés comme des grèves,
> En vous se mire mon orgueil;
> Vos vastes nuages en deuil
>
> Sont les corbillards de mes rêves,
> Et vos lueurs sont le reflet
> De l'Enfer où mon cœur se plaît.

The division of "Spleen et Idéal" is effectively closed in the 1861 edition by "L'horloge." Together with "L'héautontimorouménos" and "L'irrémédiable," two poems of the 1857 edition rearranged in the 1861 version, this poem demonstrates

---

3. Hubert, *L'esthétique des Fleurs du Mal*, p. 85. It is reasonable to agree with Hubert when he observes that "sarcophages" probably refers to the *Fleurs du Mal*.

the sharpness of Baudelaire's moral perception. After the conflicting movements of the soul have been revealed by the analysis of the poet's spiritual consciousness, Time sounds its grave and fatal warning:

Tantôt sonnera l'heure où le divin Hasard,
Où l'auguste Vertu, ton épouse encor vierge,
Où le Repentir même (Oh! la dernière auberge!)
Où tout te dira: "Meurs, vieux lâche! il est trop tard!"

The positive conception of death in the 1857 edition as a consolation to lovers, to the poor, and to artists is modified in the second edition of the *Fleurs*. In "La fin de la journée," the first of three additions made in 1861 to the division of "La mort," death is regarded as relief from both the physical and the spiritual weariness of "La Vie, impudente et criarde" which "court, danse et se tord sans raison." The poet's heart, tortured by the "songes funèbres" of spiritual anguish, craves the refreshing oblivion of non-being offered by death.

Desire for death is tempered in "Le rêve d'un curieux" by an anxiety concerning the fulfillment of the promise of repose which it offers. In a dream the poet witnesses the spectacle of his own death, savoring the exquisite horror of his separation from the world:

—J'allais mourir. C'était dans mon âme amoureuse,
Désir mêlé d'horreur, un mal particulier;

Angoisse et vif espoir, sans humeur factieuse.
Plus allait se vidant le fatal sablier,
Plus ma torture était âpre et délicieuse;
Tout mon cœur s'arrachait au monde familier.

J'étais comme l'enfant avide du spectacle,
Haïssant le rideau comme on hait un obstacle . . . .

But the curiosity of this singular audience is not satisfied by the performance. Death brings no surprising transformation:

> Enfin la vérité froide se révéla:

> J'étais mort sans surprise, et la terrible aurore
> M'enveloppait.—Eh quoi! n'est-ce donc que cela?
> La toile était levée et j'attendais encore.

This deception within the dream reflects a metaphysical anxiety which is more characteristic of a religious outlook than of skepticism. The skeptic would presumably accept as logical the idea of a void following physical extinction.

The vastness of the psychic panorama unrolled in the last of the three poems, "Le voyage," accentuates the role of death as a deliverance from the complex inferno of mortal existence —that "oasis d'horreur dans un désert d'ennui!" The final stage in the odyssey of the human soul is an escape from all that has gone before. It is an escape, moreover, to be undertaken at any price, because the unknown may reveal the lost paradise of absolute understanding:

> O Mort, vieux capitaine, il est temps! levons l'ancre!
> Ce pays nous ennuie, ô Mort! Appareillons!
> Si le ciel et la mer sont noirs comme l'encre,
> Nos cœurs que tu connais sont remplis de rayons!

> Verse-nous ton poison pour qu'il nous réconforte!
> Nous voulons, tant ce feu nous brûle le cerveau,
> Plonger au fond du gouffre, Enfer ou Ciel, qu'importe?
> Au fond de l'Inconnu pour trouver du *nouveau!*

Taken together, the additions of the 1861 edition emphasize the anguish of Baudelaire the suffering creature, rather than that of the poet. The poet, in the 1857 *Fleurs,* could still find grounds for optimism in artificial escape from the *horreur de la vie.* The satanic character of the treacherous carnal Venus and the futile consolation of autumnal love place his soul in a state of spiritual enslavement and in peril of damnation. The relentless passage of time serves to underline the theological gravity of Baudelaire's ennui. There is an urgent need for the redeeming illumination of the sublime *extase*, but the victim of the *horreur* can envisage only the termination of his present suffering in mental and physical death. In the afterlife there is at least the possibility of divine perfection, whereas terrestrial existence has produced only an unqualified spiritual void. In the penetrating analysis of his own metaphysical dilemma that Baudelaire offers in the *Fleurs du Mal,* he reflects also the moral anguish of his generation—indeed, of each succeeding generation before it comes to dishonorable terms with the imperfection of man's world. The panorama of disillusioned enthusiasms unrolled in "Le voyage" represents the human condition, with one exception. It does not admit the incidence of divine grace in human experience. From the Christian point of view, the tragedy of Baudelaire's personal existence is temporal, for the gravity of the 1861 edition of the poet's masterpiece suggests that in the final decade of his life there was an incipient awareness of his need of Grace, and in the Christian concept, the possibility of reaching God is extended into eternity.

7. The orientation of realism in Sainte-Beuve's Pensées d'août

Just as letters between Baudelaire and Sainte-Beuve have precipitated an analysis of the moral and religious aspects of anguish in the individual, as expressed in their writings, so they also suggest a relationship between the two poets' use of the city as subject matter. In a letter of January 25, 1862, Baudelaire avowed himself the "amoureux incorrigible" of one in particular of the *Poésies de Joseph Delorme*—that entitled "Les rayons jaunes." Later, in January, 1866, he referred to the Parisian flavor of certain other Delorme poems. The disciple himself thus lends authenticity to the third element suggested by Thibaudet as a formula for Sainte-Beuve's legacy to Baudelaire: he called it a "sentiment aigu de Paris." Our comparative study of poetic modernism in these two poets reveals that the effective transformation of Parisian life into the order of poetry depends upon the artist's sustained ability to distil from the diversified actuality of the metropolis the common psychological essence of man's moral anguish.

It is fair to assume that Baudelaire, while according "Les rayons jaunes" special attention, found little inspiration in the primitive synesthesia suggested by the imagery in the poem. In the spirit of his letter of 1866, he was interested in the poem rather as an attempt to chronicle the seething moral cauldron of a great metropolis. In this function the work shows considerable promise for the poetic depiction of Parisian life. The opening strophes picture the populace of the city in the leisure of Sunday evening:

> Les dimanches d'été, le soir, vers les six heures,
> Quand le peuple empressé déserte ses demeures
>   Et va s'ébattre aux champs,
> Ma persienne fermée, assis à ma fenêtre,
> Je regarde d'en haut passer et disparaître
>   Joyeux bourgeois, marchands,
>
> Ouvriers en habits de fête, au cœur plein d'aise;
> Un livre est entr'ouvert, près de moi, sur ma chaise:
>   Je lis ou fais semblant;
> Et les jaunes rayons que le couchant ramène,
> Plus jaunes ce soir-là que pendant la semaine,
>   Teignent mon rideau blanc.

After the melancholy inspired by the suggestive epithet "jaune," the observer of the metropolis turns to drown his sorrow in the crowd. With the advent of night, the city is a prey to vice:

> —Ainsi va ma pensée; et la nuit est venue;
> Je descends; et bientôt dans la foule inconnue
>   J'ai noyé mon chagrin:
> Plus d'un bras me coudoie; on entre à la guinguette,
> On sort du cabaret; l'invalide en goguette
>   Chevrotte un gai refrain.

Ce ne sont que chansons, clameurs, rixes d'ivrogne;
Ou qu'amours en plein air, et baisers sans vergogne,
       Et publiques faveurs;
Je rentre; sur ma route on se presse, on se rue;
Toute la nuit j'entends se traîner dans ma rue
       Et hurler les buveurs.

This Parisian flavor of the "Rayons jaunes" (1829) is developed in the other items which Baudelaire in the 1866 letter selected from Sainte-Beuve's poetry published between 1829 and 1838. Portions of these selected poems effectively measure his range as "poète parisien," and in juxtaposition with Baudelaire's "Tableaux parisiens" they serve to measure the younger poet's incomparably greater achievement. These poems of Sainte-Beuve are presented in the order in which they appear in the collected poetic works.

Among the *Poésies de Joseph Delorme*, the poem "La veillée" offers a contrast between the domestic felicity of the Hugo family, recently blessed in the birth of a son, and the melancholy vigil of Joseph Delorme, who, in simple charity, watches over the deathbed of a neighbor—an insignificant sufferer in the total wretchedness of the metropolis. The sinister effect of a nearby fire upon the nocturnal landscape adds to the watcher's interior depression:

Je regarde sans voir, j'écoute sans entendre;
Chaque heure sonne lente, et lorsque par trop las
De ce calme abattant et de ces rêves plats,
Pour respirer un peu je vais à la fenêtre,
(Car au ciel de minuit le croissant vient de naître),
Voilà soudain, qu'au toit lointain d'une maison,
Non pas vers l'orient, s'embrase l'horizon,
Et j'entends résonner, pour toute mélodie,
Des aboiements de chiens hurlant dans l'incendie.

In "Rose" we find a particular example of the carnal promiscuity rife in the city. The heroine is a pitiable prostitute with whom Joseph Delorme is renewing long interrupted professional ties:

> Entre les orangers, oh! qu'il fait beau, le soir,
> Se promener au frais, respirer et s'asseoir,
> Voir passer cent beautés dont le regard enivre,
> Et celles au long voile, et celles qu'on peut suivre!
> Mais, assise à deux pas, avec son œil châtain
> Et ses cheveux cendrés sur un cou de satin,
> Plus blanche que jamais bergère au pied d'un hêtre,
> Son mouchoir à la main, j'ai cru la reconnaître,
> C'est Rose. "Bonjour, Rose!—Ah! c'est vous que je vois,
> Méchant; et n'être pas venu de tout un mois!"

The gentler aspects of the Sunday evening scene in Paris, found earlier in the opening stanzas of "Rayons jaunes," are presented again, this time in a poem from the *Consolations*— "A M. Auguste le Prévost." A gloomy sunset over the Seine reminds the poet of Sundays in his childhood:

> Le soleil se couchait sous de sombres rideaux;
> La rivière coulait verte entre les radeaux;
> Aux balcons çà et là quelque figure blanche
> Respirait l'air du soir;—et c'était un dimanche;
> Le dimanche est pour nous le jour du souvenir;
> Car, dans la tendre enfance, on aime à voir venir
> Après les soins comptés de l'exacte semaine
> Et les devoirs remplis, le soleil qui ramène
> Le loisir et la fête, et les habits parés,
> Et l'église aux doux chants, et les jeux dans les prés;

The melancholy Parisian tone suggested by "Rayons jaunes" is maintained in four of the *Pensées d'août* specifically approved by Baudelaire. The first, "Dans ce cabriolet de place j'examine," is centered on the person of a repulsive old cabdriver, who represents a natural reflection of metropolitan vice. But the real source of melancholy in the poem is the fact that the exterior repulsiveness is equally matched by that of his soul, which reveals the ultimate ugliness of man's spiritual self-neglect:

Dans ce cabriolet de place j'examine
L'homme qui me conduit, qui n'est plus que machine,
Hideux, à barbe épaisse, à longs cheveux collés:
Vice et vin et sommeil chargent ses yeux soûlés.
Comment l'homme peut-il ainsi tomber? pensai-je,
Et je me reculais à l'autre coin du siège.
—Mais Toi, qui vois si bien le mal à son dehors,
La crapule poussée à l'abandon du corps,
Comment tiens-tu ton âme au dedans? Souvent pleine
Et chargée, es-tu prompt à la mettre en haleine?
Le matin, plus soigneux que l'homme d'à côté,
La laves-tu du songe épais? et dégoûté,
Le soir, la laves-tu du jour gros de poussière?
Ne la laisses-tu pas sans baptême et prière
S'engourdir et croupir, comme ce conducteur
Dont l'immonde sourcil ne sent pas sa moiteur?

The center of the second poem is a widow, newly arrived in the awesome complexity of Paris in order to watch over the early manhood of her son as he makes his career. In this work, "La voilà, pauvre mère, à Paris arrivée," the hidden vices of the metropolis are a potential threat to the simple virtue of this provincial family:

Elle n'a pas osé le laisser seul venir;
Elle le veut encor sous son aile tenir;
Elle veut le garder de toute impure atteinte,
Veiller en lui toujours l'image qu'elle a peinte
(Sainte image d'un père!), et les devoirs écrits
Et la pudeur puisée à des foyers chéris;

The third poem, "En revenant du convoi de Gabrielle," does not specify Paris, but its Parisian décor is authenticated by André Billy.[1] This composition refers to a modest funeral of a twenty-one-year-old tubercular girl, former mistress of a friend of the poet:

Quand, l'office entendu, tous deux silencieux,
Suivant du corbillard la lenteur qui nous traîne,
Nous pûmes, dans le fiacre où six tenaient à peine,
L'un devant l'autre assis, ne pas mêler nos yeux,

Et ne pas nous sourire, ou ne pas sentir même
Une prompte rougeur colorer notre front,
Un reste de colère, un battement suprême
D'une amitié si grande et dont tous parleront;

Quand, par ce ciel funèbre et d'avare lumière,
Le pied sur cette fosse où l'on descend demain,
Nous pûmes jusqu'au bout, sans nous saisir la main
Voir tomber de la pelle une terre dernière;

Quand chacun, tout fini, s'en alla de son bord,
Oh! dites! du cercueil de cette jeune femme,
Ou du sentiment mort, abîmé dans notre âme,
          Lequel était plus mort?

The last of the four poems, "Le joueur d'orgue," introduces a brother in suffering easily identifiable with those characters in Baudelaire's "Tableaux parisiens," who could on occasion touch the sublime, even in the mire of their daily wretchedness:

Tout dormait: je veillais, et, sous l'humble lumière,
Je voyais cheminer, tout près de la portière,
Un pauvre joueur d'orgue: il nous avait rejoints;
Ne pas cheminer seul, cela fatigue moins.

1. Billy, *Sainte-Beuve*, I, 180-182.

Courbé sous son fardeau, gagne-pain de misère,
Que surmontait encor la balle nécessaire,
Un bâton à la main, sans un mot de chanson,
Il tirait à pas lents, regardant l'horizon.

. . . .

Et je continuais dans mon coin à peser
Tous les maux, et, les biens, à les lui refuser.
Et par degrés pourtant blanchissait la lumière;
Son gros sourcil s'armait d'attention plus fière;
Sa main habituelle à l'orgue se porta:
Qu'attendait-il? . . . Soudain le soleil éclata,
Et l'orgue, au même instant, comme s'il eût pris flamme,
Fêta d'un chant l'aurore, et pria comme une âme.

Joseph Delorme's role as a chronicler of the Parisian scene was first suggested in the fictional biography which serves as introduction to Sainte-Beuve's first collection of verse. The pseudo-biographer observed:

Les seules distractions de Joseph, à cette époque, étaient quelques promenades, à la nuit tombante, sur un boulevard extérieur près duquel il demeurait. Ces longs murs noirs, ennuyeux à l'œil, ceinture sinistre du vaste cimetière qu'on appelle une grande ville; ces haies mal closes laissant voir, par des trouées, l'ignoble verdure des jardins potagers; ces tristes allées monotones, ces ormes gris de poussière, et, au-dessous, quelque vieille accroupie avec des enfants au bord d'un fossé; quelque invalide attardé regagnant d'un pied chancelant la caserne; parfois, de l'autre côté du chemin, les éclats joyeux d'une noce d'artisans, cela suffisait, durant la semaine, aux consolations chétives de notre ami; depuis il nous a peint lui-même ses soirées du dimanche dans la pièce des *Rayons jaunes*.

Sainte-Beuve's potential as a poet of Paris was realized only to a limited extent in the "Rayons jaunes" and the other poems quoted above. He assuredly pointed the direction, but the full realization was to be attained only later in the "Tableaux parisiens" of his more gifted disciple, who applied to the subject matter chosen from the metropolis a poetic realism peculiar to his own genius.

Sainte-Beuve also attempted a modern poetic idiom, but the direction of his new realism led him away from Parisian life into a more intimate "récit domestique et moral," which he described in the Preface to the *Pensées d'août:*

> Un mot encore pour préciser davantage le genre et la manière de ce qui suit. L'auteur a composé en tout quatre recueils de vers, dans chacun desquels, n'aimant pas trop à se répéter, il aurait voulu avoir fait quelque chose de nouveau et de distinct . . . . Dans les *Pensées d'août,* le poète, plus désintéressé, plus rassis, moins livré désormais aux confidences personelles, aurait désiré établir un certain genre moyen; développer, par exemple, l'espèce de récit domestique et moral déjà touché dans l'anecdote du vicaire John Kirkby (X^e pièce des *Consolations*), puis aussi entre-mêler certaines épîtres à demi critiques, comme celles qu'on lira adressées à M. Villemain, à M. Patin. En ajoutant aux *Pensées d'août,* dans cette réimpression, "l'Epître à Boileau" et l'anecdote de "Maria," l'auteur rentre tout à fait dans cette double pensée, et il offre, en ces deux cas du moins, un échantillon final très net de ce qu'il aurait voulu.

The author remarked that, by their moral tone, these poems were a fitting appendix and complement to his earlier *Consolations.* He was still preoccupied with an acceptable solution to the spiritual aridity of the soul, seeking an answer to the ceaseless question "Où guérir un cœur trop vite usé?" The answer seemed to him to be found in the formulae of moral discipline expounded in the first *Pensée d'août:*

> Oh! oui, ce qui pour l'homme est le point véritable,
> La source salutaire avec le rocher stable;
> Ce qui peut l'empêcher ou bien de s'engourdir
> Aux pesanteurs du corps, ou bien de s'enhardir,

S'il est grand et puissant, à l'orgueilleuse idée
Qu'il pose ensuite au monde en idole fardée
Et dans laquelle il veut à tout jamais se voir,
Ce qu'il faut, c'est à l'âme *un malheur, un devoir!*

The themes of *malheur* and *devoir*, announced in these intro-
ductory stanzas, are developed in four dramas centered upon
four instances of personal sacrifice.

Marèze, a brilliant young lawyer who finds himself at last
able to sell a lucrative practice and devote himself to a career of
public service, is thwarted in his ambition by the sudden desti-
tution of a sister and a niece. At the same time, his fortune is
dissipated by his obligations toward a widow ruined financially
by his ill-fated counsel. Securing work in a bank, Marèze assumes all his responsibilities in one comprehensive sacrifice.
The young man's devotion is rewarded by a renewal of his
Christian faith:

Il a gagné pourtant en bonheur: jusque-là,
Plus d'un mystère étrange, et que Dieu nous voila,
Avait mis au défi son âme partagée.
La vérité nous fuit par l'orgueil outragée.
Mais alors, comme au prix d'un sacrifice cher,
Sans plus qu'il y pensât en Prométhée amer,
De vertus en vertus, chaque jour, goutte à goutte,
La croyance, en filtrant, emporta tout son doute;
La persuasion distilla sa saveur,
Et la pudique foi lui souffla la ferveur.

In a second episode, the young man Doudun falls into debt
in order to provide his mother with meager comforts during
her last years. After her death, his indebtedness acts, however,
as a form of discipline against worldly temptations. He leads a
frugal and humble existence in a suburban garret, copying

music to repay his obligations. The moral of his reticent example is that duty born of a misfortune can have a salutary spiritual effect upon any distressed soul:

> Mais ce n'est pas aux doux et chastes seulement,
> Aux intègres de cœur, que contre un flot dormant
> Un malheur vient rouvrir les voiles desserrées
> Et remorquer la barque au delà des marées.
> Un seul devoir tombant dans un malheur sans fond
> Jette à l'âme en désastre un câble qui répond;
> Fait digue à son endroit aux vagues les plus hautes:
> Arrête sur un point les ruines des fautes;
> Et nous peut rattacher, en ces ans décisifs,
> Demi-déracinés, aux rameaux encore vifs.

Another drama in miniature presents Ramon de Santa-Cruz, a former officer of the Portuguese crown and an adventurer in the New World. Separated from his wife and his only son by the difficulties of his formidable temper, he is reduced to exile in Paris with an aging mother. These two relics of a former age of brilliance console each other in an atmosphere of courteous mutual devotion:

> Mais rien ne m'émut tant que lorsqu'une parole
> Soulevant quelque point d'étiquette espagnole,
> —D'étiquette de cour,—Ramon respectueux
> Se tourna vers sa mère, interrogeant des yeux.
> Oh! dans ce seul regard, muette déférence,
> Que d'éveils à la fois, quel appel de souffrance
> A celle qui savait ce pur détail royal
> Pour l'avoir pratiqué dans un Escurial!

In the concluding section of this long poem, the transcendental yearnings of the frustrated young poet, Aubignie, prove a source of anxiety for his parents. They finally reject contemptuously his uncertain pursuit of the phantom muse. Aubignie's suffering, the result of elusive poetic inspiration, could be assuaged by some more worldly responsibility, whereby he might be reached by the spirit of human charity:

> Rejoignez, s'il se peut, à des efforts moins hauts
> Quelque prochain devoir qui tire fruit des maux,
> Et d'où l'amour de tous redescende et vous gagne,
> —Afin que, revenant au soir par la campagne,
> Sans faux éclair au front et sans leurre étranger,
> Il vous soit doux de voir les blés qu'on va charger
> Et chaque moissonneur sur sa gerbe complète;

The theme of duty faithfully discharged receives its most complex treatment in a highly didactic poem of the *Pensées d'août* entitled "Monsieur Jean." The central character of this work is a dedicated rural schoolmaster whose misfortune it is to be the youngest of Jean-Jacques Rousseau's five children, abandoned like the others at a Paris orphanage soon after birth. The wealthy and influential lady who rescues him from the horrors of the orphanage is persuaded not to deny him the opportunity of learning the truth about his origin, and thereby she allows him to test the spiritual force of his character. Thereafter, necessarily involved in the general controversy over Rousseau's philosophy, the son seeks an interview with his father. The irascible old man, taking him for a spy, rebuffs his attempt at conciliation. Thus repudiated by his parent for the second time in his life, the boy sees henceforth an extensive pilgrimage of mercy as the only acceptable, because invisible, redemption of his father's sick soul. He vows to sow, in those places where his father had inspired only anger and discord, "parfum, aumône, action sûre." Monsieur Jean makes his own the martyrdom imposed on his father by the violent conflict in public opinion:

Car tout ce qui s'en dit de cher et de sacré,
D'injuste et de sanglant, amour, culte ou colère,
Qu'on l'appelle incendie ou fanal tutélaire,
Tout aboutit en lui, le déchire à la fois,
Tout crie au même instant en son âme aux abois.

. . . .

Le martyre est au comble: ainsi, pressant les coups,
Un seul cœur assemblait cette lutte de tous;
Invisible, il était l'autel expiatoire
Du génie hasardeux, la Croix de cette gloire.

In other poems of the *Pensées d'août*, the theme of duty in adversity is modified to produce a general tone of moral edification through misfortune. The work entitled "A mes amis Grégoire et Collombet" purposes to use the virtues of childhood and old age to illustrate man's constant appeal to Christian charity:

L'enfance encor, l'enfance a des vœux que j'admire,
Des élans où la foi revient luire et sourire,
Des propos à charmer les martyrs triomphants.
Et des vieillards aussi, pareils aux saints enfants,
Ont des désirs, Seigneur, de chanter ta louange,
Comme un Eliacin dans le temple qu'il range!

The charms of a child break down the social barrier between his destitute mother and a fellow prisoner, an aristocratic lady serving a purely political sentence. In the second part of the poem a retired priest's request to sing a last Christmas Mass receives the consideration due to his proved spirituality.

An element almost of moral sentimentality finds expression in "Maria," the concluding poem of the *Pensées d'août* proper. During the civil war in Portugal, a starving mother in the besieged capital is driven to offer for sale her daughter's magnificent tresses. A foreign visitor redeems the girl's locks with

his own money and is duly rewarded by the child's confidence
and gratitude:

> L'intérêt délicat qu'un regard étranger
> Marquait pour les trésors de son front en danger
> Eveilla dans son âme une aurore naissante:
> Elle se comprit belle et fut reconnaissante.
> Pour le mieux témoigner, en son charme innocent,
> La jeune fille en elle empruntait à l'enfant;
> Ses visites bientôt n'auraient été complètes
> Sans un bouquet pour moi de fraîches violettes,
> Qu'elle m'allait cueillir, se jouant des hasards,
> Jusque sous les boulets, aux glacis des remparts.

A more poignant, if less didactic, sentimentality is evidenced
in an anecdotal poem entitled "A Madame la C. de T...."
The noble lady to whom the work is addressed is asked "si
l'homme aimant, en son cœur, a puissance d'aimer comme la
femme, et s'il peut en souffrir comme elle"; her own experience leads her to answer no. Her narrative relates the embar-
rassment of a handsome young Polish exile of 1830, who un-
wittingly inspires love in a faded but not unattractive matron
belonging to a working-class German family which has sheltered and befriended him during his wanderings. At the inevitable moment when the two destinies must be separated forever, the woman offers a heart-rending picture of the suffering
inherent in love:

> Mais la femme, oh! la femme, immobile en son lieu,
> Le bras levé, tenant un mouchoir rouge-bleu
> Qu'elle n'agitait pas, je la vois là sans vie,
> Digne que, par pitié, le Ciel la pétrifie!
>
> Non, ni l'antique mère au flanc sept fois navré,
> Qui demeura debout marbre auguste et sacré,
> Ni la femme de Loth, n'égalaient en statue
> Ce fixe élancement d'une douleur qui tue!

As a faint echo of the use of mundane realism in the "Rayons jaunes," the objective reality of the countryside attracts the poet's attention in "Vœu." This poem, describing the rural scenes visible from the top of a coach, affirms the poet's function as recorder of the infinite variety of the actual in life's unceasing movement:

Que la vie en nos chants éclate ou se reflète,
La vie en sa grandeur ou sa naïveté!
Que ce vieillard assis, dont la part est complète,
Qui vit d'un souvenir sans cesse raconté;

Que la mère, et l'enfant qu'elle allaite ou qui joue,
Et celui, déjà grand, échappé de sa main,
Imprudent qui (bon Dieu!) sort de dessous la roue,
Comme un lièvre qui lève au milieu du chemin;

Que ces femmes au seuil, coquettes du village,
Et celles de la ville au cœur plus enfermé,
Tous ces êtres d'un jour nous livrent quelque gage
De ce qu'ils ont souffert, de ce qu'ils ont aimé!

It is the artist's special wish that the laughter and the tears of all human conditions may be faithfully chronicled in his poetry and that this particular talent be recognized by his fellow men.

This representative cross-section of what is significantly graphic in the realism of Sainte-Beuve's *Pensées d'août* demonstrates the restricted scope of this poet's venture into the area of poetic modernism. His original and praiseworthy plan for the creation of a modern poetry was formulated in a postscript to his *Poésies complètes*—an addition which was to have been numbered VII among the *Pensées de Joseph Delorme*:

La poésie des anciens, celle des Grecs du moins, était élevée au-dessus de la prose et de la langue courante comme un balcon. La nôtre n'a été, dès l'origine, que terre à terre et comme de rez-de-chaussée avec la prose. Ronsard et les poètes de la Renaissance ont essayé de dresser le balcon; mais ils l'ont mis si en dehors et l'ont voulu jucher si haut qu'il est tombé et eux avec lui. De là notre poésie est restée plus au rez-de-chaussée que jamais. Avec Boileau, elle s'est bornée à se faire un trottoir de deux pouces environ au-dessus de la voie commune, un promenoir admirablement ménagé; mais les trottoirs fréquentés s'usent vite, et ç'a été le cas pour le trottoir si suivi de notre poésie selon Boileau. On était revenu (sauf quelques grands mots creux) au niveau habituel et au plain-pied de la prose. Aujourd'hui il s'est agi de refaire à neuf le trottoir, et on a même visé à reconstruire le balcon.

This admirable project achieved only limited realization because the poetic direction of the "Rayons jaunes" was abandoned for a path of poignant but prosaic sentiment typical of the English Lake poets at their worst. Apart from those *Pensées d'août* to which we have ascribed a Parisian or otherwise objective realism, Sainte-Beuve's last collection of verse was composed of a pallid and formless mixture. Here were to be found shallow sonnets, original and imitated, devoted to the theme of intimate friendship; "épîtres" of a semi-critical nature; verses of adoration or nostalgia inspired by Swiss or Jura landscapes; elegies on the inevitability of time's passage and its effect on personal relationships. In spite of an appreciable affinity between the general pathos of the *Pensées d'août* and Baudelaire's sympathy for the oppressed among men, it is obvious that the ultimate refinement in pathos escaped the poet in Sainte-Beuve. With a density and penetration which increased steadily from the *Poésies de Joseph Delorme* through the *Consolations*, he had developed the powerful theme of man's essential moral duality. But he reserved his most profound statement of this theme for prose—*Volupté*—rather than for poetry. Sainte-Beuve apparently did not apply to the poetic implications of his "Rayons jaunes" the same corollary as did

Baudelaire. Either he was not able to imagine richer artistic possibilities in the analysis of sin within the social groupings of a great city, or his poetic talent was not equal to the task. The available evidence of literary history accords to Sainte-Beuve the important distinction of having foreshadowed the "Tableaux parisiens." Some twenty years of maturation were necessary for their execution by the superior genius of a brilliant disciple.

8. Modernity and the supernatural in the "Tableaux parisiens"

In confronting the essential genius of Baudelaire's poetry, we necessarily concern ourselves with some special problems related to his particular treatment of reality in artistic creation. The introduction to the present volume indicated in broad lines the poet's striving toward a poetic order of ideas. The method by which historical reality is metamorphosed into this poetic order is most easily examined in the *Fleurs* entitled "Tableaux parisiens." This analysis aids in measuring the wide difference between the final Beuvean conception of poetic realism and that of Baudelaire. Through the idiom of the *Pensées d'août*, Sainte-Beuve emphasized the pathos of certain human situations extracted from the external reality of life. This pathos, however, was more concerned with the reactions evoked in human sentiment than with the purity of man's essential moral anguish. The expression of sentiment served, in fact, as the very process of poetry. For Baudelaire, the

inspiration of the poetic process was to be defined, in his
"Notices sur Poe," by such terms as "immortel instinct du
Beau," "l'aspiration humaine vers une beauté supérieure," and
"un enthousiasme, une excitation de l'âme," but his evaluation
of Constantin Guys's scenes from Parisian low-life suggests
that he believed the most important element of poetic modernity to be moral perception. In this instance, in the capacity
of art critic, he observed:

> Et même, pour le redire en passant, la sensation générale
> qui émane de tout ce capharnaüm contient plus de tristesse
> que de drôlerie. Ce qui fait la beauté particulière de ces
> images, c'est leur fécondité morale. Elles sont grosses de
> suggestions, mais de suggestions cruelles, âpres, que ma
> plume, bien qu'accoutumée à lutter contre les représenta-
> tions plastiques, n'a peut-être traduites qu'insuffisamment.[1]

It appears possible to go even beyond Hubert's conclusions
about the supernatural orientation of Baudelaire's poetic function.[2] There seems to be a close link in the "Tableaux parisiens" between the absolute truth of poetic creation and the
spiritual tragedy of man's moral duality. Such a link serves to
illustrate the transcendental part of Baudelaire's system of
correspondences—that defined by Lloyd James Austin as symbolique—whereby finite and man-centered symbolisme is related to the divine infinity.[3] The spiritual animation, the acute
sense of life implied by the term "excitation de l'âme," is
inspired precisely by man's awareness of his own moral anguish. According to Hubert, the particular ethic of the Fleurs
du Mal always admits the existence of the moral alternative.
In Baudelaire's artistic creation the poetic function of the evil
signified in exterior reality is to suggest the theological counter-
part of that evil in man's yearning for divine perfection. Baudelaire did not deviate from the ethical unity of his masterwork

1. Baudelaire, "Le peintre de la vie moderne," Œuvres complètes, II, 627.
2. Hubert, L'esthétique des Fleurs du Mal, pp. 36-37.
3. Austin, L'univers poétique de Baudelaire, p. 55.

by venturing into the natural reality of the "Tableaux parisiens." Rather he widened the scope of that unity. The division
of "Spleen et Idéal" in the *Fleurs du Mal* is a poetic projection
of the psychic *moi* in terms of the moral duality. The majority
of the "Tableaux parisiens" are an extension and a complexity
of one *moi* in the plurality of individuals composing a metropolis. Whether or not any particular "Tableau" illuminates a
facet of man's spiritual anxiety, the poetic process of transforming the natural into the supernatural, the constantly
changing variation into the immutable absolute value, remains
the same. With minor qualifications these poems will reveal
under analysis two basic components: the décor of objective
reality, and the "merveilleux" into which this natural reality is
transformed. Without exception, the poems demonstrate that
the order of poetry is attained by the artist's creative imagination, which distils the supernatural from immediate reality.

Any plausible interpretation of "Paysage" establishes this
almost prefatory poem as a demonstration of the will to artistic creation. The sparse setting presents in "Les tuyaux, les
clochers, ces mâts de la cité" an elevated and rarefied fraction
of Paris, isolated from the main body of the metropolis. As a
result of the poetic function of idealization, this concrete
fragment of the city is supernaturally transformed into an
isolated instrument of creation. This creative part of Paris
thus becomes identified with the creative urge of the poet. The
artistic production of the city appears to be figured in "leurs
hymnes solennels," which are transported by the wind into
"les grands ciels qui font rêver d'éternité." In the lofty isolation of his garret the poet seeks absorption in the poetic
process:

> Et quand viendra l'hiver aux neiges monotones,
> Je fermerai partout portières et volets
> Pour bâtir dans la nuit mes féeriques palais.

Alors je rêverai des horizons bleuâtres,
Des jardins, des jets d'eau pleurant dans les albâtres,
Des baisers, des oiseaux chantant soir et matin,
Et tout ce que l'Idylle a de plus enfantin
L'Émeute, tempêtant vainement à ma vitre,
Ne fera pas lever mon front de mon pupitre;
Car je serai plongé dans cette volupté
D'évoquer le Printemps avec ma volonté,
De tirer un soleil de mon cœur, et de faire
De mes pensers brûlants une tiède atmosphère.

One source of poetic unity within the poem is the antithetical relation of "l'hiver aux neiges monotones" and "L'Émeute tempêtant vainement à ma vitre" to "cette volupté/ D'évoquer le Printemps avec ma volonté." Inasmuch as poetic creation always represents for Baudelaire the sublime alternative in the spiritual bipolarity, "L'Émeute" appears metaphorically to represent the profane pole of worldly temptations.

Extracts from Baudelaire's critical articles on Victor Hugo explain the dedication to him of three "Tableaux": "Le cygne," "Les sept vieillards," and "Les petites vieilles." One such paragraph emphasizes Hugo's moral perception:

Le vers de Victor Hugo sait traduire pour l'âme humaine non seulement les plaisirs les plus directs qu'elle tire de la nature visible, mais encore les sensations les plus fugitives, les plus compliquées, les plus morales (je dis exprès sensations morales) qui nous sont transmises par l'être visible, par la nature inanimée, ou dite inanimée; non-seulement, la figure d'un être extérieur à l'homme, végétal ou minéral, mais aussi sa physionomie, son regard, sa tristesse, sa douceur, sa joie éclatante, sa haine répulsive, son enchantement ou son horreur; enfin, en d'autres termes, tout ce qu'il y a d'humain dans n'importe quoi, et aussi tout ce qu'il y a de divin, de sacré ou de diabolique.[4]

4. Baudelaire, "Victor Hugo," *Œuvres complètes*, II, 477-478.

Another article examines Hugo's compassion:

> En revanche, mais par une tendance différente dont l'origine est pourtant la même, le poète se montre toujours l'*ami attendri de tout ce qui est faible, solitaire, contristé; de tout ce qui est orphelin: attraction paternelle.* Le fort devine un frère dans tout ce qui est fort, *mais voit ses enfants dans tout ce qui a besoin d'être protégé ou consolé.*[5]

Yet another extract points to Hugo's preoccupation with the supernatural in his later works:

> Mystère! La contemplation suggestive du ciel occupe une place immense et dominante dans les derniers ouvrages du poète. Quel que soit le sujet traité, le ciel le domine et le surplombe comme une coupole immuable d'où plane le mystère avec la lumière, où le mystère scintille, où le mystère invite la rêverie curieuse, d'où le mystère repousse la pensée découragée.[6]

The element of natural reality in the first poem dedicated to Hugo, "Le cygne," is furnished by an almost prosaic picture of modern Paris in the second, third, and fourth stanzas of the poem. The impression created by this décor activates the fertile creative imagination of the poet. He nullifies the immediate reality of Paris by emphasizing its instability, whereas he sees the psychic existence of the human heart, because of its stability, as possessing that absolute reality surrendered by the objective world. Baudelaire replaces the chaotic image of the natural Paris by the discipline of a poetic order founded on remembered symbols of human deprivation. In the poem the supernatural reality of memory is heightened in a crescendo of images symbolizing the distress to be found in exile:

> Je pense à mon grand cygne, avec ses gestes fous,
> Comme les exilés, ridicule et sublime,
> Et rongé d'un désir sans trêve! et puis à vous,

---

5. Baudelaire, "Les Misérables," *ibid.*, II, 569-570.
6. Baudelaire, "Victor Hugo," *ibid.*, II, 483.

Andromaque, des bras d'un grand époux tombée,
Vil bétail, sous la main du superbe Pyrrhus,
Auprès d'un tombeau vide en extase courbée;
Veuve d'Hector, hélas! et femme d'Hélénus!

Je pense à la négresse, amaigrie et phtisique,
Piétinant dans la boue, et cherchant, l'œil hagard,
Les cocotiers absents de la superbe Afrique
Derrière la muraille immense du brouillard;

A quiconque a perdu ce qui ne se retrouve
Jamais! jamais! à ceux qui s'abreuvent de pleurs
Et tettent la Douleur comme une bonne louve!
Aux maigres orphelins séchant comme des fleurs!

The personal metaphor in the final stanza of the poem is the poet's witness of his own exile in the natural reality represented by human rationality:

Ainsi dans la forêt où mon esprit s'exile
Un vieux Souvenir sonne à plein souffle du cor!

Whereas in "Le cygne" the city receives the stature of allegory, in "Les sept vieillards," second of the three "Tableaux" dedicated to Hugo, Paris becomes the actual scene of a satanic eruption. The natural reality of the surroundings presented in the first three stanzas is dissolved by scenic distortion and the investment of the metropolis with human form:

Fourmillante cité, cité pleine de rêves,
Où le spectre en plein jour raccroche le passant!
Les mystères partout coulent comme des sèves
Dans les canaux étroits du colosse puissant.

Un matin, cependant que dans la triste rue
Les maisons, dont la brume allongeait la hauteur,
Simulaient les deux quais d'une rivière accrue,
Et que, décor semblable à l'âme de l'acteur,

Un brouillard sale et jaune inondait tout l'espace,
Je suivais, roidissant mes nerfs comme un héros
Et discutant avec mon âme déjà lasse,
Le faubourg secoué par les lourds tombereaux.

The transformation of the metropolis into "colosse puissant"
identifies it with the poet's own soul, since both are receptive
to the disquieting suggestions of the supernatural "mystères."
An identification between "Le faubourg secoué par les lourds
tombereaux" and "l'esprit fiévreux et trouble" found in the
twelfth stanza of the poem suggests that both Paris and the
poet are shaken by the satanic alternative within the moral
duality implied by "mystères." Hence the enigmatic and ir-
rational spectacle of the "sept vieillards" could be interpreted
as a reminder of the seven deadly sins or at least as the poet's
own apprehension of diabolic temptations inside his spiritual
conscience.

For "Les petites vieilles," third poem in the cycle dedicated
to Hugo, the cadre of natural reality is defined in the first
stanza:

Dan les plis sinueux des vieilles capitales,
Où tout, même l'horreur, tourne aux enchantements,
Je guette, obéissant à mes humeurs fatales,
Des êtres singuliers, décrépits et charmants.

In these monstrous old crones, the actuality of their present
decrepitude is partially dissolved by the tragic antithesis of
their former existences:

Ces monstres disloqués furent jadis des femmes,
Éponine ou Laïs! Monstres brisés, bossus
Ou tordus, aimons-les! ce sont encor des âmes.

The nullification of actuality is maintained by the poet in
transformations which tend to dissolve both the femininity
and the old age of the "petites vieilles." The fourth stanza of

Part I portrays them "tout pareils à des marionnettes." They drag themselves along "comme font les animaux blessés," or they dance against their will like "pauvres sonnettes où se pend un Démon sans pitié!" Yet in the fifth stanza these ruins of humanity are endowed with "les yeux divins de la petite fille/ Qui s'étonne et qui rit à tout ce qui reluit." In the sixth stanza, the poet introduces, with dubious probability, a similar diminutiveness in the coffins holding the corpses of children and old women. In the seventh stanza, he views the frailty of these ghosts of humanity as a rebirth from death into a second infancy:

> Et lorsque j'entrevois un fantôme débile
> Traversant de Paris le fourmillant tableau,
> Il me semble toujours que cet être fragile
> S'en va tout doucement vers un nouveau berceau;

The key to the poetic function of "Les petites vieilles" is to be found in Part IV. The poetic order emerges from the confrontation of the old women's lost heroism with the unsympathetic chaos of immediate reality represented by "vivantes cités." The "ivrogne incivil" and the "enfant lâche et vil" (stanza two) fail to comprehend in these "débris d'humanité" the charms perceived by the poet—"celui que l'austère Infortune allaita." The discovery of these charms in the "plis sinueux" of the city has been the nature of Baudelaire's poetic creation. The essence of the supernatural in "Les petites vieilles" is revealed in the last three stanzas of the poem, which describe the basic moral anguish common to the psychic individuality of the poet himself and the psychic multiplicity of the "Èves octogénaires":

> Mais moi, moi qui de loin tendrement vous surveille,
> L'œil inquiet, fixé sur vos pas incertains,
> Tout comme si j'étais votre père, ô merveille!
> Je goûte à votre insu des plaisirs clandestins:

Je vois s'épanouir vos passions novices;
Sombres ou lumineux, je vis vos jours perdus;
Mon cœur multiplié jouit de tous vos vices!
Mon âme resplendit de toutes vos vertus!

Ruines! ma famille! ô cerveaux congénères!

In the "Tableau" entitled "Les aveugles" the natural reality
is that of the poet's encounter with physical blindness in the
streets of Paris. From the point of view of the natural order,
the blind are in disharmony with the normal and inspire both
horror and ridicule:

Contemple-les, mon âme; ils sont vraiment affreux!
Pareils aux mannequins; vaguement ridicules;
Terribles, singuliers comme les somnambules;
Dardant on ne sait où leurs globes ténébreux.

However, in the antithesis of the poetic order, the metaphysical anxiety of man is presented through the ambiguous alternation of physical and spiritual blindness. In accordance with
the reversed values of the supernatural, the physical deprivation of sight is transformed into the heightened spiritual perception of the meditative soul. The second quatrain of the
sonnet suggests a double quest for solar light and divine
truth:

Leurs yeux, d'où la divine étincelle est partie,
Comme s'ils regardaient au loin, restent levés,
Au ciel; on ne les voit jamais vers les pavés
Pencher rêveusement leur tête appesantie.

The moral antithesis is confirmed in the tercets. Here the
physical darkness of "le noir illimité" is affiliated with the
"silence éternel" of spiritual meditation. "Silence" provides
the moral alternative to the noisy and profane hedonism of
the metropolis "éprise du plaisir jusqu'à l'atrocité." In its
correct etymology, "atrocité" is synonymous with spiritual

blindness. By his question "Que cherchent-ils au Ciel, tous ces aveugles?" the poet-observer reveals himself "plus qu'eux hébété" by his own lack of Christian faith.

The theme of the poem "A une passante" is clearly that of an abortive encounter, but to limit the interpretation to that of a purely erotic meeting would be to miss the full signficance of the poetic order in this "Tableau." The décor of natural realism, "La rue assourdissante autour de moi," immediately suggests the hedonism of the city presented in "Les aveugles." The action "hurlait" similarly suggests the antithesis of that silence necessary to participation in the poetic order of the Absolute. The "passante," who was possibly a real person, is distinguished by traits which are reminiscent of the absolute Ideal and which seem opposed to the baseness of the multitude:

> Longue, mince, en grand deuil, douleur majestueuse,
> Une femme passa, d'une main fastueuse
> Soulevant, balançant le feston et l'ourlet;
>
> Agile et noble, avec sa jambe de statue.

In the first tercet, a moment of poetic illumination is suggested by "Un éclair," followed by a relapse into "la nuit"— the spiritual blindness of the worldly life. The elusive beauty of the supernatural Ideal, having momentarily resurrected the poet's soul, disappears into the extra-mortal sphere of eternity. This development in the tercet recalls Baudelaire's frequent preoccupation with a lost paradise—his particular manifestation of man's appetite for divine perfection. In this connection it is relevant to remember that in "Le voyage," the concluding poem of the *Fleurs du Mal* in the 1861 edition, the poet finally abandoned all hope of regaining that paradise in the mortal life. Hubert saw in the "douceur qui fascine et le plaisir qui tue" of the second quatrain an identification of the "passante" with death.[7] In offering this interpretation, he surely had in mind the liberating functions of death envisaged in "Le voyage"—"la douceur étrange de cette après-midi qui n'a jamais de fin" and "Verse-nous ton poison pour qu'il nous réconforte!" Several fleeting glimpses of the transcendental absolute indeed preceded Baudelaire's final despair—enough to convince him of an elective affinity between his mortal life and the supernatural order of reality. This affinity is affirmed in the final tercet, together with the uncertainty that its promise would ever be realized, even in the infinity of life beyond death. With or without Hubert's specific identification, the supernatural element of this poem is clearly postulated in a personal metaphysical anxiety.

The exterior reality of the "Tableau" entitled "Le squelette laboureur" is contained in the first part of the poem, which describes the subjects of cadaverous engravings to be found in the many secondhand bookstores of Paris:

Dans les planches d'anatomie
Qui traînent sur ces quais poudreux
Où maint livre cadavéreux
Dort comme une antique momie,

Dessins auxquels la gravité
Et le savoir d'un vieil artiste,
Bien que la sujet en soit triste,
Ont communiqué la Beauté.

On voit, ce qui rend plus complètes
Ces mystérieuses horreurs,
Bêchant comme des laboureurs,
Des Écorchés et des Squelettes.

The supernatural order of poetry operates in the second part of the poem, where a metaphysical anxiety is formulated concerning the peace to be found beyond the grave:

7. Hubert, p. 184.

Dites, quelle moisson étrange,
Forçats arrachés au charnier,
Tirez-vous, et de quel fermier
Avez-vous à remplir la grange?

Voulez-vous (d'un destin trop dur
Épouvantable et clair emblème!)
Montrer que dans la fosse même
Le sommeil promis n'est pas sûr;

Qu'envers nous le Néant est traître;
Que tout, même la Mort, nous ment, . . .

In "Le voyage" the poet is primarily concerned with an issue
from the despair of mortal ennui. An issue is sought at any
price—"Plonger au fond du gouffre, Enfer ou Ciel, qu'importe?"—and the range of this price is precisely the range of
man's spiritual duality. The metaphysical anxiety expressed
in the present poem is concerned with one term of the duality
—Enfer. The moral alternative of the duality provides the
answer to the question: "et de quel fermier avez-vous à remplir
la grange?" This alternative term of the duality finds formal
expression in a *Fleur* composed at least as early as 1857 and
entitled "La Rançon":

Pour rendre le juge propice,
Lorsque de la stricte justice
Paraîtra le terrible jour,

Il faudra lui montrer des granges
Pleines de moissons, et des fleurs
Dont les formes et les couleurs
Gagnent le suffrage des Anges.

The supernatural transformation into the order of poetry
is achieved in the poem "Danse macabre" by the ambiguity
of the "squelette." In its dual nature, this guest of the "fête

de la vie" symbolizes both physical death and a summons to spiritual rebirth. Actual reality is represented by the totality of the worldly "fête servile." To those who celebrate it, the "squelette" appears as a caricature of life's reality:

> Aucuns t'appelleront une caricature,
> Qui ne comprennent pas, amants ivres de chair,
> L'élégance sans nom de l'humaine armature.
> Tu réponds, grand squelette, à mon goût le plus cher!

The elegance of the human frame—ineffable or anonymous, according to the interpretation of the ambiguity—is dependent upon the spiritual suggestivity of a corpse. In the inevitable and common fact of death, man's vanity is dissolved. The compulsion of the ambiguous "vivante carcasse" to attend the "fête de la vie" imparts to the ball the nature of an infernal "sabbat du Plaisir." The connection, in the seventh and eighth stanzas of the poem, of such symbols as "ton cauchemar moqueur," "l'enfer allumé dans ton cœur," "De l'antique douleur éternel alambic!" and "l'insatiable aspic" evokes the goading consciousness of original sin in every meditative soul. But how many celebrators are worthy of the spiritual salvation promised by the sure prospect of corporal death:

> Pour dire vrai, je crains que ta coquetterie
> Ne trouve pas un prix digne de ses efforts;
> Qui, de ces cœurs mortels, entend la raillerie?
> Les charmes de l'horreur n'enivrent que les forts!
>
> Le gouffre de tes yeux, plein d'horribles pensées,
> Exhale le vertige, et les danseurs prudents
> Ne contempleront pas sans d'amères nausées
> Le sourire éternel de tes trente-deux dents.

Inasmuch as they fail to notice "la trompette de l'Ange sinistrement béante ainsi qu'un tromblon noir," the "danseurs prudents" demonstrate only a false discretion. In a final ambiguity, the "squelette" assumes the role of spectator before the revelers, who now imitate the "coquetterie" of a spiritual death. The last four stanzas of the poem turn the invective against the dancers in Death's apostrophe:

> Bayadère sans nez, irrésistible gouge,
> Dis donc à ces danseurs qui font les offusqués:
> "Fiers mignons, malgré l'art des poudres et du rouge,
> Vous sentez tous la mort! O squelettes musqués,
>
> Antinoüs flétris, dandys à face glabre,
> Cadavres vernissés, lovelaces chenus,
> Le branle universel de la danse macabre
> Vous entraîne en des lieux qui ne sont pas connus!
>
> Des quais froids de la Seine aux bords brûlants du Gange,
> Le troupeau mortel saute et se pâme, sans voir
> Dans un trou du plafond la trompette de l'Ange
> Sinistrement béante ainsi qu'un tromblon noir.
>
> En tout climat, sous tout soleil, la Mort t'admire
> En tes contorsions, risible Humanité,
> Et souvent, comme toi, se parfumant de myrrhe,
> Mêle son ironie à ton insanité!"

The "fête servile" has become a caricature of absolute reality. As he establishes the order of poetry in "Danse macabre" by this reversal of values, Baudelaire offers a justification of total poetry.

In the poem "L'amour du mensonge," the basic formula of the "Tableaux parisiens," whereby a natural reality is transformed into the supernatural order of poetry, undergoes a variation. The natural reality of this "Tableau" is introduced and defined by the philosophical reflection in the fifth stanza:

> Je sais qu'il est des yeux, des plus mélancoliques,
> Qui ne recèlent point de secrets précieux;

Beaux écrins sans joyaux, médaillons sans reliques,
Plus vides, plus profonds que vous-mêmes, ô Cieux!

The fact of this actuality—"ta bêtise ou ton indifférence"—is elaborated by Baudelaire himself in his *Choix de maximes consolantes sur l'amour:*

> La bêtise est souvent l'ornement de la beauté; c'est elle qui donne aux yeux cette limpidité morne des étangs noirâtres, et ce calme huileux des mers tropicales. La bêtise est toujours la conservation de la beauté; elle éloigne les rides; c'est un cosmétique divin qui préserve nos idoles des morsures que la pensée garde pour nous, vilains savants que nous sommes![8]

But it is the destiny and function of poetry, remarks Baudelaire elsewhere, to nullify actuality: "C'est une grande destinée que celle de la poésie! Joyeuse ou lamentable, elle porte toujours en soi le divin caractère utopique. Elle contredit sans cesse le fait, à peine de ne plus être."[9] The contradiction of the factual "bêtise" by the creative imagination of the poetic order thus becomes the "mensonge" of the poem. In contrast to the naïve sterility of the "bêtise," the third stanza emphasizes the emotional maturity and sagacity of autumnal love:

> Je me dis: Qu'elle est belle! et bizarrement fraîche!
> Le souvenir massif, royale et lourde tour,
> La couronne, et son cœur, meurtri comme une pêche,
> Est mûr, comme son corps, pour le savant amour.

Another poem, "Semper eadem," proclaims the need for the "mensonge"; for the "fête de la vie" is unbearable when "notre cœur a fait une fois sa vendange" and death exerts a more subtle attraction than life.

By exception, the order of poetry in "Rêve parisien" does not reflect so dramatically man's moral anguish. Yet the essential duality of human nature is clearly expressed by the

8. Baudelaire, *Œuvres complètes,* I, 182.
9. Baudelaire, "Pierre Dupont," *ibid.,* I, 432-433.

natural and supernatural elements in the poem. The intolerable ennui of Parisian actuality is described only in the last two stanzas of the "Tableau":

> En rouvrant mes yeux pleins de flamme
> J'ai vu l'horreur de mon taudis,
> Et senti, rentrant dans mon âme,
> La pointe des soucis maudits;

> La pendule aux accents funèbres
> Sonnait brutalement midi,
> Et le ciel versait des ténèbres
> Sur le triste monde engourdi.

The natural ugliness of the city is transformed into a supernatural Paris by the creative imagination operating entirely inside the artist. The double aspect of this transformation is explained by Chérix in his commentary on the poem:

> Le point de vue surnaturel, le parti pris mystique de Baudelaire lui impose en outre le soin de traduire, par des symboles appropriés, les touches de l'au-delà dont les rêves sont les truchements. C'est de cette double élaboration, celle de l'âme visitée par les songes, et celle de l'esprit ordonnateur des images, qu'est sorti le *Rêve parisien*.[10]

The interpreting dream effects the penetration into mortal awareness of an infinite system of symbols—*la symbolique*. It is the function of the poet, his consciousness animated by dream, to translate the figures of the *symbolique* into the appropriate symbols of a man-centered *symbolisme*—the "analogie universelle" within the grasp of mortal imagination. The shaping of this series of inferior images is performed by the poet's intellect. Baudelaire himself described as "hiéroglyphique" the particular kind of dream which projects the supernatural into the natural.[11] In the order of poetry, the aesthetic

10. Chérix, *Commentaire des Fleurs du Mal*, p. 366.
11. Baudelaire, "Le poème du haschisch," *Œuvres complètes*, II, 259-260.

stylization of a supernatural Paris produces a landscape devoid of the "végétal irrégulier":

> Et, peintre fier de mon génie,
> Je savourais dans mon tableau
> L'enivrante monotonie
> Du métal, du marbre et de l'eau.
>
> Babel d'escaliers et d'arcades,
> C'était un palais infini,
> Plein de bassins et de cascades
> Tombant dans l'or mat ou bruni;
>
> Et des cataractes pesantes,
> Comme des rideaux de cristal,
> Se suspendaient, éblouissantes,
> A des murailles de métal.
>
> Non d'arbres, mais de colonnades
> Les étangs dormants s'entouraient,
> Où des gigantesques naïades,
> Comme des femmes, se miraient.

It is notable that the wonders of this artificial scenery shine with a "feu personnel" in the absence of solar light. There is also a supernatural dissociation of noise—"un silence d'éternité"—from the movement in the picture.

In spite of Baudelaire's own engulfment in the abyss of human suffering, his compassion derives more from moral lucidity than from humanitarian sentiment. Through his acute sense of personal sin, he shares as an individual in the metaphysical anxiety of man, which is universalized in the "Tableaux parisiens." This spiritual anguish is activated by the sober confrontation of the profane pole in the moral duality. Hence, his Parisian poems are neither an objective description of the metropolis nor a social commentary on urban life. They present rather the diversified examples of the profane abounding in the natural reality of the city. The "Tableaux parisiens" preserve the aesthetic unity of true *Fleurs du Mal* only insofar as they suggest the alternate and sublime pole in man's dual nature. As "Les petites vieilles" so well illustrates, the psychic life of the poet himself is reflected in the triumphs and failures which comprise the modern heroism of Paris and her populace.

9. *Baudelaire's* Petits poëmes en prose— *Poetry and charity*

According to Baudelaire's letter of January 15, 1866, the spirit of Joseph Delorme was apparent not only in the "Tableaux parisiens" of the *Fleurs du Mal,* but also in his *Petits poëmes en prose,* which bore the subtitle *Spleen de Paris.* As evidence of the close relationship between Baudelaire's two chronicles of Parisian life, the first four verses of the epilogue to the poet's prose poems clearly reaffirm the essential poetic function of the *Fleurs:*

> Le cœur content, je suis monté sur la montagne
> D'où l'on peut contempler la ville en son ampleur,
> Hôpital, lupanars, purgatoire, enfer, bagne
>
> Où toute énormité fleurit comme une fleur.[1]

The poet's achievement in both works is a projection of the individual psychic *moi* through the souls inhabiting Paris. The

1. Baudelaire, "Petits poëmes en prose," *Œuvres complètes,* I, 993.

best and most frequently cited items in the *Spleen de Paris* suggest a conception of modern heroism similar to that conveyed by Baudelaire in his "Tableaux parisiens." The order of poetry is founded on the same sense of spiritual animation— an extended *ribote de vitalité*—that transcends the sordid reality of the metropolis.

In these exquisite prose poems, which are inspired by human or animal characters observed on the Parisian scene, Baudelaire chronicles the common man's normal pursuit of his humble destiny. Modern Adam and Eve are depicted in the suffering of their daily struggle with hardship, in their illusions, in the satisfaction of their material needs and sensuous desires, in their automatic response to the call of routine duties. In his chronicles the author is necessarily concerned with the cripples of this world, both the physically afflicted and the downcast in spirit. Besides evoking his compassion, the experiences of the citizens of Paris enhance Baudelaire's own consciousness of the horrors of life. He suspects, too, that these lame souls share with him a heroic aspiration to the sublime.

Baudelaire explains in the prose poem "Les veuves" that the poet of modernity disdains as source of his inspiration the "turbulence dans le vide" represented by the happiness of the fortunate. Such a poet's field of interest lies rather in the suffering victims of the *horreur de la vie*. In this particular composition the author credits Vauvenargues with a description situating the *veuves* in their characteristic milieu and emphasizing their nature as cripples:

Vauvenargues dit que dans les jardins publics il est des allées hantées principalement par l'ambition déçue, par les inventeurs malheureux, par les gloires avortées, par les cœurs brisés, par toutes les âmes tumultueuses et fermées, en qui grondent encore les soupirs d'un orage, et qui reculent loin du regard insolent des joyeux et des oisifs. Ces retraites ombreuses sont les rendez-vous des éclopés de la vie.

The substance of poetic creation, Baudelaire continues, is to be found in the facts or legends comprising the universal drama of human existence:

> Un œil expérimenté ne s'y trompe jamais. Dans ces traits rigides ou abattus, dans ces yeux caves et ternes, ou brillants des derniers éclairs de la lutte, dans ces rides profondes et nombreuses, dans ces démarches si lentes ou si saccadées, il déchiffre tout de suite les innombrables légendes de l'amour trompé, du dévouement méconnu, des efforts non récompensés, de la faim et du froid humblement, silencieusement supportés.

A similiar conception of the true poetic substance is revealed in "Les bons chiens," where *bons* is equated with *pauvres* or *crottés*. In this prose poem the composer invokes the aid of a less fastidious and bolder muse to help him portray the outcasts of the animal world:

> Arrière la muse académique! Je n'ai que faire de cette vieille bégueule. J'invoque la muse familière, la citadine, la vivante, pour qu'elle m'aide à chanter les bons chiens, les pauvres chiens, les chiens crottés, ceux-là que chacun écarte, comme pestiférés et pouilleux, excepté le pauvre dont ils sont les associés, et le poète qui les regarde d'un œil fraternel.

He rejects the pampered pets of the privileged classes to embrace the more valid pedigree of suffering:

> A la niche, tous ces fatigants parasites!
> Qu'ils retournent à leur niche soyeuse et capitonnée!
> Je chante le chien crotté, le chien pauvre, le chien sans domicile, le chien flâneur, le chien saltimbanque, le

chien dont l'instinct, comme celui du pauvre, du bo-
hémien et de l'histrion, est merveilleusement aiguillon-
né par la nécessité, cette si bonne mère, cette vraie
patronne des intelligences!

The humble citizenry of the capital periodically seeks respite
from the crushing struggle against the maleficent powers of
life. In "Le vieux saltimbanque" Baudelaire achieves a particularly dramatic effect by depicting the extreme misery of a
decrepit old entertainer against the ebb and flow of the populace, who attempt to assuage their defeats in the frantic gaiety
of the carnival: "Partout la joie, le gain, la débauche; partout
la certitude du pain pour les lendemains; partout l'explosion
frénétique de la vitalité. Ici la misère absolue, la misère affu-
blée, pour comble d'horreur, de haillons comiques, où la nécessité, bien plus que l'art, avait introduit le contraste."

In the midst of plenty, the accusing faces of the needy inspire in the fortunate either shame or embarrassed annoyance.
The heart of those who indulge in the pleasures of luxury is
sometimes softened toward the wretched. But this tenderness
is not necessarily communicable; "Les yeux des pauvres" reveals how, at a certain elegant new café, the seed of hatred is
sown between two lovers because of a compassion that the
couple do not share. The six eyes which are the innocent cause
of the quarrel symbolize for Baudelaire the perpetual drama
of the éclopés of Paris:

> Droit devant nous, sur la chaussée, était planté un
> brave homme d'une quarantaine d'années, au visage
> fatigué, à la barbe grisonnante, tenant d'une main un
> petit garçon et portant sur l'autre bras un petit être trop
> faible pour marcher. Il remplissait l'office de bonne et
> faisait prendre à ses enfants l'air du soir. Tous en gue-
> nilles. Ces trois visages étaient extraordinairement
> sérieux, et ces six yeux contemplaient fixement le café

nouveau avec une admiration égale, mais nuancée diversement par l'âge.

For the common people death is the only permanent release from the progressive martyrdom of spiritual erosion imposed by the daily physical struggle, but there are temporary reliefs. In "Le crépuscule du soir," the approach of night brings relaxation from monotonous drudgery: "Le jour tombe. Un grand apaisement se fait dans les pauvres esprits fatigués du labeur de la journée; et leurs pensées prennent maintenant les couleurs tendres et indécises du crépuscule." The citizens enslaved on the relentless treadmill of passing time may otherwise relieve their burdens in the oblivion afforded by the various intoxicants recommended in the prose poem "Enivrez-vous":

> Pour ne pas sentir l'horrible fardeau du Temps qui brise vos épaules et vous penche vers la terre, il faut vous enivrer sans trêve.
> Mais de quoi? De vin, de poésie ou de vertu, à votre guise.

Moreover, the struggling masses are not subject to despair. In "Chacun sa chimère," each traveler bears willingly the burden of his own cherished illusion, which impels him to pursue his gloomy destiny:

> Chacun d'eux portait sur son dos une énorme Chimère, aussi lourde qu'un sac de farine ou de charbon, ou le fourniment d'un fantassin romain . . . . Tous ces visages fatigués et sérieux ne témoignaient d'aucun désespoir; sous la coupole spleenétique du ciel, les pieds plongés dans la poussière d'un sol aussi désolé que ce ciel, ils cheminaient avec la physionomie résignée de ceux qui sont condamnés à espérer toujours.

In extracting his poetic substance from the diffuse chronicle of human ills, Baudelaire remains faithful in the *Petits poèmes en prose* to the aesthetic principle of his *Fleurs du Mal*. He seeks what is potentially sublime in the atrociously abnormal. Two examples from the Parisian prose poems illustrate his technique. In "Mademoiselle Bistouri," the case history of what conventional society would regard as a very unhealthy prostitution of the flesh yields a glimpse of the divine omnipresence which serves as a key to Baudelaire's poetic intention:

> Quelles bizarreries ne trouve-t-on pas dans une grande ville, quand on sait se promener et regarder? La vie fourmille de monstres innocents.—Seigneur, mon Dieu! vous, le Créateur, vous, le Maître; vous qui avez fait la loi et la liberté; vous, le souverain qui laissez faire, vous, le juge qui pardonnez; vous qui êtes plein de motifs et de causes, et qui avez peut-être mis dans mon esprit le goût de l'horreur pour convertir mon cœur, comme la guérison au bout d'une lame; Seigneur, ayez pitié, ayez pitié des fous et des folles; O Créateur! peut-il exister des monstres aux yeux de Celui-là seul qui sait pourquoi ils existent, comment ils *se sont faits* et comment ils auraient pu *ne pas se faire*?

In "Le joujou du pauvre," the atrocious live rat is the unforgettable symbol of the sublime, drawn albeit from the squalor of raw life. This terrible plaything brings happiness to the innocent "marmot-paria" and is coveted by the rich boy stifled in the boredom of artificial luxury. Through the iron barrier of a garden railing this shared interest draws together two widely separated social beings into a common humanity.

Some among the *Petits poèmes en prose* do not participate in the external projection of ennui effected in Baudelaire's chronicle of the Parisian populace. In one group of introspective compositions the background of the metropolis provides a psychological décor for the author's personal spleen. This atmosphere sharpens his consciousness of the duality in which his own soul alternates between the *horreur* and the *extase* of man's experience. In "La chambre double," the poet's ecstatic dream of an ideal paradise—equivocal gift, perhaps, of some treacherous narcotic—is interrupted by the entry of a ghost. This specter symbolizes the destruction of the spirit wrought by the anguish of earthly existence: "C'est un huissier qui vient me torturer au nom de la loi; une infâme concubine qui vient crier misère et ajouter les trivialités de sa vie aux douleurs de la mienne; ou bien le saute-ruisseau d'un directeur de journal qui réclame la suite du manuscrit." With the specter reappears tyrannical Time, bringing his satanic retinue of memories, regrets, fears, anxieties, nightmares, anger, and neuroses. The poet is shocked out of his languid dream world to confront the sinister squalor of his actual abode.

> Oui! ce taudis, ce séjour de l'éternel ennui, est bien le mien. Voici les meubles sots, poudreux, écornés; la cheminée sans flamme et sans braise, souillée de crachats, les tristes fenêtres où la pluie a tracé des sillons dans la poussière; les manuscrits, raturés ou incomplets; l'almanach où le crayon a marqué les dates sinistres!

In "A une heure du matin," the victim of spleen seeks in the solitude of his apartment an escape from the horrors of the day's routine. There he meditates upon the shortcomings of other men and upon his own vile acts or omissions:

> Horrible vie! Horrible ville! Récapitulons la journée: avoir vu plusieurs hommes de lettres, dont l'un m'a demandé si l'on pouvait aller en Russie par voie de terre (il prenait sans doute la Russie pour une île); avoir disputé généreusement contre le directeur d'une revue, qui à chaque objection répondait: "C'est ici le parti des honnêtes gens," ce qui implique que tous les autres

journaux sont rédigés par des coquins; avoir salué une vingtaine de personnes, dont quinze me sont inconnues; avoir distribué des poignées de main dans la même proportion, et cela sans avoir pris la précaution d'acheter des gants; être monté pour tuer le temps, pendant une averse, chez une sauteuse qui m'a prié de lui dessiner un costume de Vénustre; ... m'être vanté (pourquoi?) de plusieurs viles actions que je n'ai jamais commises, et avoir lâchement nié quelques autres méfaits que j'ai accomplis avec joie; délit de fanfaronnade, crime de respect humain; ... ouf! est-ce bien fini?

Another composition, "Le mauvais vitrier," reveals what kind of unreasoning madness may be born in the spiritual desert of ennui. The victim of a pathological or satanic practical joker is the entirely fortuitous exterior target of an interior spirit of destruction:

Un matin, je m'étais levé maussade, triste, fatigué d'oisiveté, et poussé, me semblait-il, à faire quelque chose de grand, une action d'éclat; et j'ouvris la fenêtre, hélas! ... La première personne que j'aperçus dans la rue, ce fut un vitrier dont le cri perçant, discordant, monta jusqu'à moi à travers la lourde et sale atmosphère parisienne. Il me serait d'ailleurs impossible de dire pourquoi je fus pris, à l'égard de ce pauvre homme, d'une haine aussi soudaine que despotique.

The moral enormity of this incident is intensified by the fact that the crime itself affords but a moment of perverse enjoyment to the perpetrator.

The atrocious impulses and abject moods of personal spleen suggest, however, the spiritual alternative in the potential ecstasy of the sublime. In "A une heure du matin," the poet, in order to banish "le mensonge et les vapeurs corruptrices du monde," invokes the spiritual intercession of his loved ones.

To restore his battered self-respect, he begs the divine gift of poetic creativity. In similar tone, the same night which in "Le crépuscule du soir" brings a respite in the struggle of the harried workingman brings also to the poet a sweet deliverance from the anguish of the day. His soul regains its liberty in a supernatural world of imagination and, perhaps, artistic inspiration.

Baudelaire unfolds in his prose poems a drama peopled by characters the essence of whose heroism is their total engagement in the anguish of spiritual bipolarity. Their author presents them in the midst of their sordid struggles with the evil forces of man's world—in temptation and in sin—but he conveys the impression that they never surrender the essential nobility which is their heritage from the Divine Creator. Their immersion in the horror of earthly existence does not drown their aspiration toward the sublime, and they are always open to the visitation of God's grace. The heroic type is well illustrated by the decrepit old woman of "Un cheval de race":

> Elle est vraiment laide; elle est fourmi, araignée, si vous voulez, squelette même; mais aussi elle est breuvage, magistère, sorcellerie! en somme, elle est exquise .... Usée peut-être, mais non fatiguée, et toujours héroïque, elle fait penser à ces chevaux de grande race que l'œil du véritable amateur reconnaît, même attelés à un carrosse de louage ou à un lourd chariot.

In "Les veuves," the poet draws a striking contrast between one of his heroines and the triviality of her surroundings. The occasion is a military band concert, and at first the author finds incredible the presence of such a noble character among the poor, who greedily feast upon the entertainment from beyond the barrier:

> C'est toujours chose intéressante que ce reflet de la joie du riche au fond de l'œil du pauvre. Mais ce jour-

là, à travers ce peuple vêtu de blouses et d'indienne, j'aperçus un être dont la noblesse faisait un éclatant contraste avec toute la trivialité environnante.

C'était une femme grande, majestueuse, et si noble dans tout son air, que je n'ai pas souvenir d'avoir vu sa pareille dans les collections des aristocratiques beautés du passé. Un parfum de hautaine vertu émanait de toute sa personne. Son visage, triste et amaigri, était en parfaite accordance avec le grand deuil dont elle était revêtue . . . . Pourquoi donc reste-t-elle volontairement dans un milieu où elle fait une tache si éclatante?

But harsh economic necessity has forced this respectable widow to forego a privileged seat, for the sake of a son whose needs are her sole concern: "La grande veuve tenait par la main un enfant comme elle vêtu de noir; si modique que fût le prix d'entrée, ce prix suffisait peut-être pour payer un des besoins du petit être, mieux encore, une superfluité, un jouet." The prose poem "Les bons chiens" portrays the drama of creatures moved by carnal instincts, material needs, and a sense of duty. The heroic role of these characters is their very pursuit of their particular destiny, with seeming resignation to the changing adversities of their environment:

> Rendez-vous d'affaires, rendez-vous d'amour. A travers la brume, à travers la neige, à travers la crotte, sous la canicule mordante, sous la pluie ruisselante, ils vont, ils viennent, ils trottent, ils passent sous les voitures, excités par les puces, la passion, le besoin ou le devoir. Comme nous ils se sont levés de bon matin, et ils cherchent leur vie ou courent à leurs plaisirs.

The obvious compassion of the poet for the sufferings of his fellow "parias" is not however blind to the need for a drastic psychotherapy in order to dispel the dangerous inferiority complex produced by their habitual dejection. The beggar in

"Assommons les pauvres" has to be provoked into proving himself worthy of the respect which society has so long denied him. He is given a sense of his dignity by the "énergique médication" of his retaliation to physical affront. The therapist offers him constructive advice for the future: " 'Monsieur, *vous êtes mon égal!* Veuillez me faire l'honneur de partager avec moi ma bourse; et souvenez-vous, si vous êtes réellement philanthrope, qu'il faut appliquer à tous vos confrères, quand ils vous demanderont l'aumône, la théorie que j'ai eu la *douleur* d'essayer sur votre dos.' "

Baudelaire most clearly explains the poetic essence of his *Petits poèmes en prose* when he comments in "Les foules" on the rare privilege enjoyed by the poet of modernity:

> Le poète jouit de cet incomparable privilège, qu'il peut à sa guise être lui-même et autrui. Comme ces âmes errantes qui cherchent un corps, il entre, quand il veut, dans le personnage de chacun . . . . Le promeneur solitaire et pensif tire une singulière ivresse de cette universelle communion. Celui-là qui épouse facilement la foule connaît des jouissances fiévreuses, dont seront éternellement privés l'égoïste, fermé comme un coffre, et le paresseux, interné comme un mollusque. Il adopte comme siennes toutes les professions, toutes les joies et toutes les misères que la circonstance lui présente.

To create the poetry of Paris, continues the author, is to participate in an indescribable orgy, in a "sainte prostitution" of the spirit, which gives itself entirely, poetry and charity, to the unforeseen incidental reality and to the passing stranger. Artistic creation and love of fellow man are thus joined in the poet's tribute to the "éclopés de la vie."

Through this spiritual prostitution that takes place in the "bain de multitude," the poet lives and suffers in personalities other than his own. For example, in the sordid degradation of his "vieux saltimbanque" he perceives the reflection of his own probable destiny:

> Et, m'en retournant, obsédé par cette vision, je cherchai à analyser ma soudaine douleur, et je me dis: Je viens de voir l'image du vieil homme de lettres qui a survécu à la génération dont il fut le brillant amuseur; du vieux poète sans amis, sans famille, sans enfants, dégradé par sa misère et par l'ingratitude publique, et dans la baraque de qui le monde oublieux ne veut plus entrer!

The metropolis is full of similar stories, factually authentic, and of legends, true only in the artist's imagination. It does not matter, writes Baudelaire in "Les fenêtres," whether the incidental reality exterior to himself is true or untrue, providing that it gives him a keener awareness of his own existence and a deeper understanding of the purpose of that existence in a creation unlimited in time or space.

The order of poetry in Baudelaire's *Petits poèmes en prose* is effectively summarized by a remarkable coincidence of meaning evidenced in three passages chosen from different prose poems. The last stanza of the epilogue to the collection confirms the author's strong conviction concerning the rich poetic material offered by Parisian life:

> Je t'aime, ô capitale infâme! Courtisanes
> Et bandits, tels souvent vous offrez des plaisirs
> Que ne comprennent pas les vulgaires profanes.

The poet of modernity has the special gift of sensitivity to the spiritual drama inherent in the exterior reality of the metropolis. We are reminded in "Les foules" that many human beings do not share this poetic perception: "Il est bon d'apprendre quelquefois aux heureux de ce monde, ne fût-ce que pour humilier un instant leur sot orgueil, qu'il est des bonheurs supérieurs au leur, plus vastes et plus raffinés." The tragedy of popular insensitivity is as widespread, suggests Baudelaire, as the human race. As for Paris, the fatuous vulgarity of the common mind seems to him well characterized by the encounter in "Un plaisant" between the irresponsible reveller and the harassed, but obedient, donkey:

> L'âne ne vit pas ce beau plaisant, et continua de courir avec zèle où l'appelait son devoir.

> Pour moi, je fus pris subitement d'une incommensurable rage contre ce magnifique imbécile, qui me parut concentrer en lui tout l'esprit de la France.

The drunkard is insulated by his intoxication from the spiritual current of the human drama. The animal, on the contrary, symbolizes those human beings who, in accepting the ferocious challenge of worldly horror, create their own particular roles in heroic patience and endurance.

10. Conclusion

The charge of insincerity leveled in some quarters against Baudelaire for hailing the Delorme poems as *"Les Fleurs du Mal* de la veille" cannot be adequately substantiated merely by citing his need for favorable criticism and moral justification in the face of official and private condemnation. The possibility of some calculated self-interest in his sustained quest for Sainte-Beuve's approval of the *Fleurs* is too obvious to require discussion. There are also testimonies of affinity which, by reason of their timing, have no obvious connection with the furthering of a professional triumph. For example, Baudelaire's epistle in verse addressed to Sainte-Beuve in 1844 is clearly a tribute of naïve enthusiasm rather than a calculating bid for attention. Again, the admiration and sense of obligation expressed in Baudelaire's letter of January, 1866, suggest a retrospective evaluation rendered in the lucid gravity of his last years. Historically, in spite of any measure of calculation which may actually have existed in Baudelaire's approach to Sainte-Beuve, competent Baudelairean scholarship in our century has reconfirmed the essential significance of the 1865 testimony. Whether he believed it or not, in that testimony the younger poet imputed to both his own poems and those of Sainte-Beuve a theological meaning through his use of the paradox, a "flower of evil." What Baudelaire may or may not have truly appreciated in 1865 has been established subsequently by the analysis of the relevant texts.

To clarify the poetic affinity between Baudelaire and Sainte-Beuve—an affinity which has been obscured by the brevity and superficiality of critics' comments—it is useful to return once more to Thibaudet's formula defining the legacy. However, the logical development of their poetic creation necessitates a rearrangement of the three elements: first *intelligence critique*; second, *christianisme intérieur*; and third, *sentiment aigu de Paris*. Psychological perspicacity thus precedes theological enlightenment, and an analysis of these two elements is far more indicative of a poetic legacy than is the transmission of any *sentiment aigu de Paris*.

Baudelaire's *intelligence critique* undoubtedly appreciated Sainte-Beuve's penetrating analysis of his own psychological dilemma in the fictitious Delorme. In the *Poésies de Joseph Delorme*, the lyrical quality of the elder poet depends upon the most intimate soundings of a *mal du siècle* which never entirely ceased to influence his life. This personal agony, fictitiously projected in the sufferings of his hero, assumes a conscious pattern in the poem "Le songe," which, though inferior to Baudelaire's "Le voyage," performs a similar function as the psychological panorama of a *vie insuffisante*. In the light of Baudelaire's aesthetic aims in the *Fleurs du Mal*, one may confidently assume that he discerned in Delorme's inner conflict at least the outline of a spiritual duality alternating between a profane and a sublime pole.

By the same psychological experiences, Delorme and the individual identifiable in the *Fleurs du Mal* pursue similar false ecstasies and founder in the same spiritual abyss that results from the disintegration of these artificial paradises. However, the balance of psychological bipolarity is not completely identical. In the Delorme poems, the function of the *élégie analytique* typified by "Causerie au bal" and "Contredanse" is to register the delicate progression of disillusion which leads to the hero's psychological collapse. He reaches a state of utter deprivation, bewildered by his own wretchedness, and does not recognize the machinations of satanic evil as the cause of his suffering. In the 1857 edition of Baudelaire's *Fleurs*, on the contrary, a very strong postulation of evil is contained in the prefatory poem "Au lecteur" and "Bénédiction." This is reinforced in the 1861 edition by "Hymne à la Beauté," as well as other poems added to the cycle of "Spleen et Idéal." Thus, while it is clear that he understood the theological implication of a *Fleur du Mal*, there is no evidence in the Delorme poems that Sainte-Beuve had a similar awareness. The result of this difference is that the same psychological themes, which appear to compose only a naïve autobiography in the Delorme poems, seem like universalized tableaux of evil in Baudelaire's masterpiece.

The lack of aesthetic unity in the Delorme collection makes it difficult to apply to them a uniformly clear pattern of psychological bipolarity. However, they provided for Baudelaire, as he informed Sainte-Beuve in 1844, an introduction to the elder poet's novel *Volupté*. The formal structure of this genre permitted a much more sharply delineated and much more evenly balanced pattern of moral duality. The author's declared psychological objective in the confession of his hero, Amaury, was to analyze the corruption by human perversity of a supernatural gift. For Baudelaire, the important feature of Amaury's character was certainly the awareness of a fundamental interior disharmony between conflicting moral tendencies. The hero's critical intelligence was able in retrospect to simplify the psychological multivalence as a basic division of the soul, alternating between the attractions of the finite and the infinite.

With Sainte-Beuve the *christianisme intérieur* of Thibaudet's formula appears as the theological interpretation of the moral schism already established by Delorme's critical faculty. The author's conclusion in the *Consolations* is that only through the discipline and the immutable forms of the Christian religion can Delorme's taste for life be recovered and the fulness of an earthly *vie suffisante* be attained. This second collection of Sainte-Beuve's poems offers a translation in Christian terms of the purely psychological confusion inherent in the *mal de la jeunesse*. The *horreur de la vie* becomes the spiritual frustration caused by the absence of God in Delorme's life. The *extase* is now the aspiration of a contrite Delorme toward God. Christian theology defines the psychological dualism of man anew, as an alternation between sin and divine beatitude. Hence, the most serious aspect of sensual indulgence is the risk of damnation for the soul.

In Sainte-Beuve's *Volupté* the priesthood provides the remedy for Amaury's spiritual collapse. The Christian insight of a resurrected Amaury gives a divine purpose to the sufferings of his spiritual disintegration. The sacrifice to God of his *vie insuffisante* is the means of redemption in a new and entirely satisfying religious life. In penetrating the essential Christian paradox of purification through suffering, the erstwhile sinner encounters yet another essential principle of Catholic theology, that the resurrection of man's fallen spirit comes as a direct intervention of God's grace. Piety now becomes a co-operative achievement between Amaury's mortal will and the Holy Spirit.

These theological principles concerning the roles of suffering and divine grace in Amaury's redemption are in significant harmony with the truncated Christianity of the *Fleurs du Mal*. The crux of the *intelligence critique* in Baudelaire's masterpiece, as we have already indicated, is a firm postulation of evil as the foundation of the *horreur de la vie*. Baudelaire appears, in the poem "Bénédiction," to regard the suffering produced by the imperfections of man's world as a divine instrument of spiritual purification:

Soyez béni, mon Dieu, qui donnez la souffrance
Comme un divin remède à nos impuretés
Et comme la meilleure et la plus pure essence
Qui prépare les forts aux saintes voluptés!

Suffering, born of man's sin, thus becomes a link between the profane and sublime poles of man's spiritual duality.

Jean Massin maintains that the suffering expressed in Baudelaire's artistic creation is defective, if judged as truly Christian sacrifice, since it is not explicitly related to the supreme sacrifice of Christ.[1] Certainly there are only four references to God the Son in the *Fleurs du Mal*, and few, if any, elsewhere in his other writings. Sainte-Beuve, apart from his history of Port-Royal, is equally poor in New Testament inspiration. We should thus be surprised if either poet had gone on to produce Christian poetry on the order of Verlaine's "Sagesse" or comparable to the work of Paul Claudel or Charles Péguy. In the *Fleurs* of 1861, the torment involved in the various cycles of disillusion is brought to its maximum intensity in the concluding poems of "Spleen et Idéal." The whole tone of despair which terminates the second edition suggests the theological urgency which is formally expressed in "L'horloge." This urgency, which is in keeping with the Catholic principle of redemption through suffering, is Baudelaire's real contribution to an atmosphere of *christianisme intérieur*. The constant emphasis upon satanic evil in man's sin,

1. Massin, *Baudelaire "entre Dieu et Satan,"* pp. 99 and 114.

and upon the anguish which derives from it, automatically suggests the moral alternative of beatitude through God's grace. This implication is the theological essence of the *Fleurs du Mal* and, at least for Baudelaire, lies at the heart of man's metaphysical dilemma.

In the lyrical works of both poets, the critical faculty and Christian enlightenment actually combine to produce, in the pattern of spiritual bipolarity, a rigid interpretation of the contemporary moral anguish. So far, Thibaudet's formula appears substantially valid. It is, however, doubtful whether Sainte-Beuve's conviction as to the truth of this interpretation survived the influence of Lamennais. The principal theme of the *Pensées d'août* published in 1838 is no longer the moral duality of man's soul. The theological insipidness of this collection of poems breaks the aesthetic unity of the Beuvean lyric legacy and raises many questions as to the meaning of the *sentiment aigu de Paris*. Baudelaire, by contrast, maintains the aesthetic unity of the spiritual duality throughout the division of "Tableaux parisiens" in his *Fleurs* of 1861, making each of them—and many of his later prose poems as well—conform substantially to the theological nature of a *Fleur du Mal*. That is to say, each tableau was required to reflect that spiritual dualism of man which is the basis of his metaphysical anguish. The immediate reality of Parisian life was thus only an extension of the author's personal *vie insuffisante*. The horror of metropolitan sin must continue to suggest the moral alternative by the transformation of natural, hence sinful, reality into the supernatural reality of poetry. In each Parisian poem, Baudelaire made the suffering produced under the modern conditions of a great city function as the link between the profane and the sublime, bridging the vast gap between finite imperfection and the perfection of the divine infinity.

Whereas the "Rayons jaunes" was a true precursor of "Crépuscule du soir," Sainte-Beuve's range as a poet of Paris, in the

Baudelairean sense, was restricted. Of the Beuvean compositions which the younger poet selected for particular praise, not more than six Parisian poems can be said to develop the promise of the "Rayons jaunes" by engagement in the contemporary moral anguish. The break in aesthetic unity and the theological weakness apparent in the *Pensées d'août* are the direct result of Sainte-Beuve's decision to give a new orientation to the intimate realism of his poetry. The majority of the poems in this collection sound a note of moral edification which, while reminiscent of the English Lake poets, is very far from the theological virility of *Volupté* and from the ultimate pathos of suffering in Baudelaire's Parisian heroes.

Both poets possessed a keen flair for detecting the profane pole of man's duality in the sordid moral and material conditions of the metropolis. Nevertheless, it is obvious that the poetic meaning of the immediate reality largely eluded Sainte-Beuve and but rarely found expression in his poems. Therefore, the importance of the Parisian element in Thibaudet's formula must be considerably qualified. The analysis of the *sentiment aigu de Paris* leads inevitably to a consideration of the true nature of lyricism and its relation to modernity in poetry; for it is precisely in this area that the most disturbing divergence is revealed in the poetic objectives of Sainte-Beuve and Baudelaire.

Sainte-Beuve's significant contribution to a modern poetry was foreshadowed in what he intended to be the seventh *Pensée* of Joseph Delorme, but what was in fact the postscript to his collected poetical works. His ambition, as therein announced, was to raise poetry above its traditional level of equality with prose—even to the level advocated by the Pléiade. Since his relatively sickly muse restricted him to the prosaic themes of vulgar life, he was faced with the task of extracting the quintessence of poetic meaning from that very vulgarity. His formal poetics, embracing the principle of the universal analogy and its relation to the divine unity, promised considerable success in this ambition. In the physiological and psychological disturbances of Delorme and Amaury, Sainte-Beuve analyzed with the most lucid critical faculty the delicate components of the spiritual anguish in his age. The richness and refinement of his details indeed offered an innovation in the literature of the Romantic agony. His analysis of the metaphysical dilemma in contemporary man was, moreover, framed in a consciously theological interpretation of the divisive forces in man's soul. But in the *Pensées d'août* he halted the practical application of his poetic theory begun in *Volupté* and the earlier poetry by giving a new orientation to the intimate realism of his lyricism. What he really effected was a theological reorientation, in which the virile theology of sin and its concomitant suffering was replaced by a vaguely Christian compulsion to duty and service. The theological urgency of man's spiritual anguish was foreshortened into a passionless and didactic sentimentality aroused by the prosaic chronicle of economic and social depression. The ultimate successor to this type of lyricism was François Coppée rather than Charles Baudelaire.

For Baudelaire, indeed, the essence of poetic modernity was theological intelligence—a particular intelligence that, ironically enough, he might readily have gleaned, and probably did glean, from Amaury and Delorme. What is ageless in man's creation and earthly experience—the dual postulation of the human spirit—was given a new meaning by the events of the Old and New Testaments. In the deeper Christian view of history, modernity in all of man's culture began with the Crucifixion and Resurrection of Christ. Sainte-Beuve found it convenient to forget this truth in the scientism of the mid-century. Happily for his poetic intensity, Baudelaire never ceased to live this metaphysical anguish in his art and in his personal existence.

The paradox of eternal Christian values in shifting contemporary culture provides the key to the poetic modernity of Baudelaire. In his critical articles on the visual arts, he emphasized the double composition of beauty, dividing it always into the absolute and relative elements. The passion, or *couleur*, of his heroes joined each of them, through sin and suffering, to the ageless spiritual paradox of man. According to Baudelaire, the modern conception of art prescribed the creation of a suggestive magic which would include simultaneously the object and the subject, the immediate reality exterior to the artist and the inner reality of the artist himself. Exterior reality, interpreted by the symbolic imagination of the artist, is raised to the supernatural level of the Divine Absolute, which is the seat of all meaning. The hidden catalyst in the elevation is the poet's Christian awareness of suffering as the theological link between separation from God in sin and reunion with Him in salvation. The passion of modernity was understood by Baudelaire as an ardent engagement in the Christian anguish of duality.

Bibliography

Selected works of Charles Baudelaire

Juvenilia, œuvres posthumes, reliquiae. Edited by Jacques Crépet.
3 vols. Paris: Louis Conard, 1939-1952.
Les Fleurs du Mal. Edited by Jacques Crépet and Georges Blin.
Paris: José Corti, 1942.
Œuvres complètes. 2 vols. Paris: Le Club du Meilleur Livre, *Le
Nombre d'Or*, 1955.

Selected works of Charles-Augustin Sainte-Beuve

Portraits de femmes. 2nd ed. Paris: Garnier Frères, 1852.
Les Causeries du Lundi. Vol. XI. Paris: Garnier Frères, 1857-1872.
Les Causeries du Lundi. Vol. XVI: *Table générale et analytique.*
Edited by Ch. Pierrot. Paris: Garnier Frères, 1880.
Poésies complètes. 2nd ed. revised. Paris: G. Charpentier, 1890.
Volupté. Paris: G. Charpentier, 1890.

[213]

Les Nouveaux Lundis. Vol. I. Paris: Calmann Lévy, 1890.

Vie, Poésies et Pensées de Joseph Delorme. Edited by Gérald Antoine, with notes. Paris: Nouvelles Editions Latines, 1956.

Selected correspondence

Baudelaire, Charles. *Correspondance générale: 1833-1866.* Compiled, classified and annotated by Jacques Crépet. 6 vols. Paris: Louis Conard, 1947-1953.

Hugo, Victor. *Correspondance: 1815-1835.* Paris: Calmann Lévy, 1896.

———. *Correspondance: 1836-1882.* Paris: Calmann Lévy, 1898.

Sainte-Beuve, Charles-Augustin. *Correspondance: 1822-1865.* 2 vols. Paris: Calmann Lévy, 1877-1878.

———. *Correspondance générale: 1815-1846.* Compiled, classified and annotated by Jean Bonnerot. 6 vols. Paris: Librairie Stock, 1935-1949.

Selected printed works

Austin, Lloyd James. *L'univers poétique de Baudelaire: symbolisme et symbolique.* Paris: Mercure de France, 1956.

Bandy, W. T. *Répertoire des Écrits sur Baudelaire.* Madison, Wis.: Privately printed, 1953.

Billy, André. *Sainte-Beuve, sa vie et son temps.* Vol. I: *Le romantique, 1804-1848.* Paris: Flammarion, 1952.

———. *Sainte-Beuve, sa vie et son temps.* Vol. II: *L'épicurien, 1848-1869.* Paris: Flammarion, 1952.

Blin, Georges. *Baudelaire.* Paris: Gallimard, 1939.

Bonnerot, Jean. *Un demi-siècle d'études sur Sainte-Beuve. 1904-1954.* Paris: Société d'édition "Les Belles Lettres," 1957.

Charpentier, John. *Évolution de la poésie lyrique de Joseph Delorme à Paul Claudel.* Paris: Œuvres représentatives, 1930.

Chérix, Robert-Benoît. *Commentaire des Fleurs du Mal.* Geneva: P. Cailler, 1949.

Crépet, Eugène. *Ch. Baudelaire.* Paris: Albert Messein, 1928.

Ferran, André. *L'esthétique de Baudelaire*. Paris: Hachette, 1933.

Fondane, Benjamin. *Baudelaire et l'expérience du gouffre*. Paris: Séghers, 1947.

Hubert, Judd David. *L'esthétique des Fleurs du Mal*. Geneva: P. Cailler, 1953.

Lamartine, Alphonse de. *Méditations poétiques*. Edited by Paul Vernière. Paris: Delmas, 1949.

Massin, Jean. *Baudelaire "entre Dieu et Satan."* Paris: René Julliard, 1945.

Prévost, Jean. *Baudelaire*. Paris: Mercure de France, 1953.

Ruff, Marcel A. *Baudelaire: l'homme et l'œuvre*. Paris: Hatier-Boivin, 1955.

————. *L'esprit du mal et l'esthétique baudelairienne*. Paris: Armand Colin, 1955.

————. "Notules baudelairiennes," *Revue d'Histoire littéraire de la France*, 51ᵉ année (1951), pp. 483-486.

Smith, Maxwell Austin. *L'influence des Lakistes sur les romantiques français*. Paris: Jouve et Cie, 1920.

Thibaudet, Albert. *Histoire de la littérature française de 1789 à nos jours*. Paris: Librairie Stock, 1936.

Vandérem, Fernand. *Baudelaire et Sainte-Beuve*. Paris: H. Leclerc, 1917.

Vouga, Daniel. *Baudelaire et Joseph de Maistre*. Paris: José Corti, 1957.

Index

Consolations

Pensées d'août

Baudelaire's poems cited in text

Juvenilia

Fleurs du mal

Petits poèmes en prose

General

Héautontimorouménos, characterization as a, 124
Hubert, Judd David, 16, 93, 97, 113, 130, 173, 181-82
Hugo, Adèle (Madame Victor), 56
Hugo, Victor, 6, 7, 10, 41, 47, 48, 157, 175-76, 177, 178

Intelligence critique, 18, 204, 207

Jansenist, 73, 82, 137
Juvenilia, by Baudelaire, 86

Lamartine, Alphonse de, 6, 39, 41, 49
Lamennais, Félicité de, 208
La Rochefoucauld, François de, 56
Lesbian adventure, a, 129
Lesbianism, 130
Lesbos, 131
Limbes, Les, by Baudelaire, 11, 45, 84, 86, 88, 89, 91, 92, 93, 97, 100, 101
Limbo, 66
Lost paradise, 104-5, 106, 128, 136, 142, 143, 148, 151, 154, 181, 196
Lucifer, 133

Maistre, Joseph de, 38
Malade du siècle, 43
Mal de la jeunesse, 206
Mal du siècle, 20, 22, 44, 45, 204
Mallarmé, Stéphane, 134
"Marmot-paria," 195, 199
Mariette (nurse to Baudelaire), 126
Massin, Jean, 15, 56, 207
Méricourt, Théroigne de, 149
"Merveilleux," the; *see* Supernatural, the
Messager de L'Assemblée, Le, 88
Michelangelo, 54
Midas, 151
Milton, John, 134
Modern anguish, 11, 17, 43, 45, 86, 88
Modern heroism, 13, 100, 189, 191; *see also* Modernity, heroism of
Modern idiom, in Saint-Beuve, 163, 169
Modernism, poetic, 12, 15, 136, 156, 169; *see also* Modernity
Modernity: poetry of, 11; Baudelaire's definition of, 12-13; heroism of, 87; poetic, 173, 210, 211; poet of, 191, 200, 201; in poetry, 209; Christian view of, 210; passion of, 211; *see also* Modern heroism

Nerval, Gérard de, 134
Nieri, Sisina (Madame), 150
"Nostalgie de l'arrière-monde," 105
Notices sur Poe, by Baudelaire, 173

Objective correlative, 89
Olivier, Juste, 55
Original sin, 58, 93, 137, 184

"Parias"; *see* "Marmot-paria"
Paris: profane sophistication of, 76; promiscuous encounters in, 81; evil in, 125; idealized presentation of, 126; artistic inspiration in, 140; *see also* Supernatural Paris
Parnassian, 107
Pascal, Blaise, 93
Péguy, Charles, 207
Pensées de Joseph Delorme, Les, by Sainte-Beuve, 14
Perspicacity, moral, 83, 130
Pluto, 119
Poe, Edgar Allan, 14
Porte Saint-Martin Theatre, 104
Port-Royal, 73, 82, 207
Prarond, Ernest, 11, 86, 107, 118
Prévost, Jean, 17
Proserpine, 118-19

Racine, Jean, 73
"Récit domestique et moral," in Sainte-Beuve, 163
Reversibility, 38, 113, 137
Revue de Paris, La, 89
Revue des Deux Mondes, La, 84, 100
Revue Française, La, 85, 106, 110
Ribote de vitalité, 191
Rimbaud, Arthur, 134
Rousseau, Jean-Jacques, 166
Ruff, Marcel A., 17, 44, 84, 86, 97, 106, 128, 134, 135

Sabatier, Apollonie (Madame), 102-4, 108-10, 121-22, 132, 137, 146, 147, 150
Saint Anthony, 131; *see also* "Tentation de saint Antoine"
"Sainte prostitution," 200
"Saintes voluptés," 29
Saint-Martin, Louis-Claude, 72, 73
Salon de 1846, Le, by Baudelaire, 12-13
Salon de 1859, Le, by Baudelaire, 13
Sapphic passion, the, 130
Sara la Juive, 118
Satan: temptation by, 101, 108; machinations of, 111; light extinguished by, 112; point of view of, 131; affinity between poet and, 133; Milton's, 134
Sentiment aigu de Paris, 18, 156, 204, 208, 209
Shakespeare, William, 41
Smith, Maxwell Austin, 8
Supernatural, the: as "merveilleux" in Baudelaire, 13, 16; tendency of artist towards, 14; voices of, 24, 37; ecstasy projected into, 112; suffering related to, 113; man naturally drawn to, 131; idealism related to, 132; poetic function of, 173; distilled from immediate reality, 174; Hugo's preoccupation with, 176; essence of, 179; reversed values in, 180; projected into the natural, 187; and the imagination, 198
Supernatural destiny of the poet, 112
Supernatural dissociation of noise, 188
Supernatural gift of *volupté*, 205